T0299826

MACAT

An Analysis of

Stanley Milgram's

Obedience to Authority
An Experimental View

Mark Gridley
with
William J. Jenkins

ROUTLEDGE

Published by Macat International Ltd
24:13 Coda Centre, 189 Munster Road, London SW6 6AW.

Distributed exclusively by Routledge
2 Park Square, Milton Park, Abingdon, Oxon OX14 4RN
711 Third Avenue, New York, NY 10017, USA

Routledge is an imprint of the Taylor & Francis Group, an informa business

www.macat.com
info@macat.com

Cataloguing in Publication Data
A catalogue record for this book is available from the British Library.
Library of Congress Cataloguing-in-Publication Data is available upon request.
Cover illustration: Etienne Gilfillan

ISBN 978-1-912303-64-9 (hardback)
ISBN 978-1-912127-24-5 (paperback)
ISBN 978-1-912282-52-4 (e-book)

Notice

CONTENTS

THE MACAT LIBRARY

The Macat Library is a series of unique academic explorations of seminal works in the humanities and social sciences – books and papers that have had a significant and widely recognised impact on their disciplines. It has been created to serve as much more than just a summary of what lies between the covers of a great book. It illuminates and explores the influences on, ideas of, and impact of that book. Our goal is to offer a learning resource that encourages critical thinking and fosters a better, deeper understanding of important ideas.

Each publication is divided into three Sections: Influences, Ideas, and Impact. Each Section has four Modules. These explore every important facet of the work, and the responses to it.

This Section-Module structure makes a Macat Library book easy to use, but it has another important feature. Because each Macat book is written to the same format, it is possible (and encouraged!) to cross-reference multiple Macat books along the same lines of inquiry or research. This allows the reader to open up interesting interdisciplinary pathways.

To further aid your reading, lists of glossary terms and people mentioned are included at the end of this book (these are indicated by an asterisk [*] throughout) – as well as a list of works cited.

Macat has worked with the University of Cambridge to identify the elements of critical thinking and understand the ways in which six different skills combine to enable effective thinking.
Three allow us to fully understand a problem; three more give us the tools to solve it. Together, these six skills make up the **PACIER** model of critical thinking. They are:

ANALYSIS – understanding how an argument is built
EVALUATION – exploring the strengths and weaknesses of an argument
INTERPRETATION – understanding issues of meaning

CREATIVE THINKING – coming up with new ideas and fresh connections
PROBLEM-SOLVING – producing strong solutions
REASONING – creating strong arguments

To find out more, visit **WWW.MACAT.COM.**

CRITICAL THINKING AND *OBEDIENCE TO AUTHORITY*

Primary critical thinking skill: CREATIVE THINKING
Secondary critical thinking skill: REASONING

Stanley Milgram is one of the most influential and widely-cited social psychologists of the twentieth century. Recognized as perhaps the most creative figure in his field, he is famous for crafting social-psychological experiments with an almost artistic sense of creative imagination – casting new light on social phenomena in the process.

His 1974 study *Obedience to Authority* exemplifies creative thinking at its most potent, and controversial. Interested in the degree to which an "authority figure" could encourage people to commit acts against their sense of right and wrong, Milgram tricked volunteers for a "learning experiment" into believing that they were inflicting painful electric shocks on a person in another room. Able to hear convincing sounds of pain and pleas to stop, the volunteers were told by an authority figure – the "scientist" – that they should continue regardless. Contrary to his own predictions, Milgram discovered that, depending on the exact set up, as many as 65% of people would continue right up to the point of "killing" the victim.

The experiment showed, he believed, that ordinary people can, and will, do terrible things under the right circumstances, simply through obedience. As infamous and controversial as it was creatively inspired, the "Milgram experiment" shows just how radically creative thinking can shake our most fundamental assumptions.

ABOUT THE AUTHOR OF THE ORIGINAL WORK

Stanley Milgram was born in 1933 to a Jewish immigrant family in New York City. A gifted student, he earned a PhD in psychology from Harvard; he joined the psychology faculty first at Yale, then at Harvard, before spending the rest of his career at the City University of New York. Like many of his generation, Milgram was deeply affected by the Holocaust, and haunted by the question as to how so many Germans and others could have participated in such an unimaginable crime. His whole career focused on exploring obedience and conformity. Milgram died in 1984 of a heart attack, aged 51.

ABOUT THE AUTHORS OF THE ANALYSIS

Dr Mark Gridley teaches psychology at Heidelberg University, Ohio. His research interests include social psychology and the history and psychology of music.

Dr Bill Jenkins holds a PhD in psychology from the University of Michigan. He is currently co-chair of the Department of Psychology at Mercer University.

ABOUT MACAT

GREAT WORKS FOR CRITICAL THINKING

Macat is focused on making the ideas of the world's great thinkers accessible and comprehensible to everybody, everywhere, in ways that promote the development of enhanced critical thinking skills.

It works with leading academics from the world's top universities to produce new analyses that focus on the ideas and the impact of the most influential works ever written across a wide variety of academic disciplines. Each of the works that sit at the heart of its growing library is an enduring example of great thinking. But by setting them in context – and looking at the influences that shaped their authors, as well as the responses they provoked – Macat encourages readers to look at these classics and game-changers with fresh eyes. Readers learn to think, engage and challenge their ideas, rather than simply accepting them.

'Macat offers an amazing first-of-its-kind tool for interdisciplinary learning and research. Its focus on works that transformed their disciplines and its rigorous approach, drawing on the world's leading experts and educational institutions, opens up a world-class education to anyone.'

Andreas Schleicher
Director for Education and Skills, Organisation for Economic Co-operation and Development

'Macat is taking on some of the major challenges in university education … They have drawn together a strong team of active academics who are producing teaching materials that are novel in the breadth of their approach.'

Prof Lord Broers,
former Vice-Chancellor of the University of Cambridge

'The Macat vision is exceptionally exciting. It focuses upon new modes of learning which analyse and explain seminal texts which have profoundly influenced world thinking and so social and economic development. It promotes the kind of critical thinking which is essential for any society and economy. This is the learning of the future.'

Rt Hon Charles Clarke, former UK Secretary of State for Education

'The Macat analyses provide immediate access to the critical conversation surrounding the books that have shaped their respective discipline, which will make them an invaluable resource to all of those, students and teachers, working in the field.'

Professor William Tronzo, University of California at San Diego

WAYS IN TO THE TEXT

KEY POINTS

- Stanley Milgram (1933–84) was an American psychologist* best known for his work on obedience to authority; psychology is the study of the ways in which the mind determines our behavior.

- *Obedience to Authority* describes 24 experiments that show how ordinary people will follow the commands of an authority, even if this involves inflicting pain on someone else.

- The book reflects on how society is organized around social hierarchies—structures decided by degrees of status—that use obedience to maintain efficient functioning.

Who Was Stanley Milgram?

Stanley Milgram, the author of *Obedience to Authority: An Experimental View* (1974), was born to Jewish immigrant parents in 1933 and grew up in New York City. His parents and teachers recognized that he was an extremely intelligent, creative, and curious person. After high school he enrolled at Queens College, a public institution in New York City, where he majored in political science*—the study of political behavior and institutions—and minored in art. Milgram wrote two musicals that were not produced. He also wrote poetry and children's books.

Milgram earned a PhD in psychology from Harvard University, during which he conducted studies in two European countries, Norway and France, on conformity* (the impulse to behave and think in a way that "fits in" with the majority). His first academic job was at Yale University as an assistant professor in 1961; there he designed and conducted experiments looking at people's obedience to authorities who demand that they inflict pain on others. This was less than two decades after World War II.* Milgram was trying to help understand why ordinary Germans participated in the torture and killing of millions of Jews in Europe between 1933 and 1945.

Milgram left Yale after his obedience studies, returned to Harvard from 1963 to 1966, and then spent the remainder of his career at the City University of New York. There he investigated why subway and bus users will give their seats to others and how city dwellers form mental maps of their cities. He also explored the claim that people are linked to others by way of chains of acquaintances—that we are separated by no more than six degrees from almost anyone else.[1]

Milgram died in 1984.

What Does *Obedience to Authority* Say?

Milgram's 1974 book *Obedience to Authority* summarized studies of more than a thousand participants. Ordinary people were told they were administering painful electric shocks as part of an experiment to measure the effects of punishment on learning and memory; Milgram recorded and analyzed their behavior.

The key result, which came as a surprise to most readers, was that 40 to 65 percent of participants obeyed the experimenter's demands to administer a 450-volt (potentially lethal) shock to a participant, even if that person complained of a heart condition, or screamed in pain.

While the shock generator was fake, such results provided a compelling parallel to the Holocaust* of 1941 to 1945, during which many thousands of Germans, Poles, Ukrainians, Romanians, Estonians, and others obeyed the Nazi* authorities in helping to round up and murder six million Jews, in addition to gypsies, homosexuals, and members of other groups. (The Nazi Party was the extreme right-wing political party that led Germany into World War II.) Millions more, conditioned by anti-Semitism* (a centuries-old hatred of Jews in majority Christian societies), and fearful of the Nazis, stood by quietly as their Jewish neighbors were dragged away to their deaths.

Milgram and many commentators saw the results of his studies as scientific proof for the existence of a basic human tendency: ordinary people tend to obey authorities. This is true even when those authorities demand actions that conflict with personal conscience. This allows normal people to go along with orders that will hurt their fellow human beings.

Many scholars believe that revealing this tendency can help us understand how ordinary and socially "normal" people enabled Germany's Nazi leaders to carry out their horrific plans. Milgram's book was written at the height of the Vietnam War,* during which the United States fought in Asia with the aim of limiting the spread of the political system of communism.* Many academics believe Milgram's studies also cast light on why, on various occasions, American soldiers massacred noncombatant men, women, and children during that brutal conflict in the 1960s and early 1970s.[2]

Why Does *Obedience to Authority* Matter?

Milgram thought the Holocaust could not have been carried out by the Nazis alone. Thousands of ordinary citizens must have been obeying orders to help implement the atrocities, even though such actions violated their morals. Milgram wondered whether such extensive obedience reflected long-established cultural traditions among the German people—traditions of following rules and obeying orders. So he set up experiments in which he recruited ordinary people to see how far they would obey an authority when it required inflicting pain on others.

He observed such remarkable compliance by ordinary citizens in the United States that he came to believe such obedience was not restricted to German people. It was, rather, a basic aspect of human nature.

Milgram believed his volunteers were able to violate their own morals because they had handed over responsibility for their actions to the authority of the experimenter who prodded them. He believed this mirrored the trust the German people had placed in the Nazi authorities during the Holocaust. This finding remains relevant today, because individuals continue to be placed in situations where other people will die needlessly if they do not challenge authority.

There are various examples of this type of behavior. For instance, for many years cigarette manufacturers chemically treated tobacco to make it more addictive; some of the chemicals used can cause cancer. Yet they denied doing this, even in testimony before the United States Congress. They demanded that their employees suppress such information, and they ruined the life and career of at least one company chemist who revealed it to the news media.[3]

Similarly, media reports have shown how drug companies have suppressed unwanted findings from clinical trials for new psychoactive drugs[4]—drugs that affect the mental state of those taking them. Then they marketed the drugs with misleading promises, claiming that they were much more effective than placebos (pills that do not contain medicine, but are prescribed for their psychological effect).

If ordinary people can follow orders to hurt their fellow human beings, we need to know what situations and attitudes promote such obedience so that we can prevent future atrocities. We need to know how to help people challenge authority, especially when orders conflict with personal values and conscience. To these ends we can benefit from in-depth knowledge about how results of the study differed according to variations in its design. Milgram's explanations of his results can also help us to understand the potentially destructive effects of obedience to authority.

For these reasons, the obedience studies are presented in almost every introductory psychology text, and are examined in depth in every social psychology* textbook.

NOTES

1   Judith Kleinfeld, "Six Degrees of Separation: Urban Myth?" *Psychology Today* 35, no. 2 (March/April 2002): 74; and Stanley Milgram, "The Small World Problem," *Psychology Today* 1, no. 1 (1967): 60–7.

2   Albert Bandura, "Selective Moral Disengagement in the Exercise of Moral Agency," *Journal of Moral Education* 31, no. 2 (2002): 101–19.

3   Marie Brenner, "The Man Who Knew Too Much," *Vanity Fair*, May 1996, accessed May 15, 2016, http://www.vanityfair.com/magazine/1996/05/wigand199605.

4   David Teather, "Spitzer Forces Glaxo to Publish Drug Trials," *Guardian*, August 27, 2004, accessed May 15, 2016, http://www.theguardian.com/business/2004/aug/27/mentalhealth.glaxosmithklinebusiness.

SECTION 1
INFLUENCES

MODULE 1
THE AUTHOR AND THE HISTORICAL CONTEXT

KEY POINTS

- *Obedience to Authority* is important because it not only helps explain the actions of Nazi* collaborators during the Holocaust* (during which many millions of people, most of whom were Jewish, were industrially murdered), but also reveals an aspect of human nature.

- As a child, Milgram was exposed to people who had suffered during the Holocaust.

- Milgram was familiar with important social psychology* research on conformity* and obedience.

Why Read This Text?

Stanley Milgram's *Obedience to Authority: An Experimental View* (1974) is one of the most widely known studies aimed at understanding how regular people are capable of committing heinous crimes, such as those carried out during the Holocaust.

Psychologists* generally focus on personality traits to explain behavior. Historians, political scientists* (those engaged in the study of political behavior), and social psychologists (those engaged in the study of the role of the mind in social behavior) focus more on social and political forces. Even before the end of World War II* (1939–45), social psychologists had been trying to identify trends in human behavior that could help to explain genocide in Europe.

Like many social psychologists who came before him, Milgram was Jewish. As a child growing up in America, he had known refugees from Europe who reported experiences that were so awful that they

> **❝** My interest in obedience is purely personal, and concerns the fact that many of my friends and relatives were badly hurt by other men who were simply following orders. **❞**
>
> Stanley Milgram Papers, Yale University Library

begged explanation. After becoming a research psychologist, he went beyond earlier work in the field and came up with new laboratory experiments. These were designed to study various types of situations that might parallel the obedience and conformity found among those who helped carry out the Holocaust.

In his book, Milgram explained how his findings mirror what still happens in the world wherever military forces operate, especially when soldiers massacre noncombatants. Because atrocities continue to occur today, his findings and his reflections about them remain relevant. Moreover, Milgram felt he had identified central aspects of human nature, not just forces that explain certain atrocities. *Obedience to Authority*, therefore, continues to be one of the most important studies in the field of psychology.

Author's Life
Milgram was born to Jewish immigrant parents in 1933 and grew up in New York City. When he was a child, his parents hosted Jewish refugees from Europe in their house. He attended Queens College in New York, majoring in political science and minoring in art. Milgram intended to work as a foreign service officer for the Department of State, but became unhappy with the largely philosophical approach of political science.

A friend introduced him to psychology and he switched to this discipline for his PhD at Harvard University. As part of his doctoral research, he ran studies in Norway and France on conformity,* which he defined as "the action of a subject when he goes along with his peers, people of his own status, who have no special right to direct his behavior."[1] The next step in his program of research would be to study obedience, which he defined as "the action of the subject who complies with authority."[2]

The importance of the Holocaust for Milgram's work cannot be overstated. In his introduction to *Obedience to Authority*, he wrote, "It has been reliably established that, from 1933 to 1945, millions of innocent people were systematically slaughtered on command. Gas chambers were built, death camps were guarded, and daily quotas of corpses were produced with the same efficiency as the manufacture of appliances. These inhumane policies may have originated in the mind of a single person but they could only have been carried out on a massive scale if a very large number of people obeyed orders."[3]

As a result, he began investigating people's tendency to follow orders, even when commands conflict with morals.

Author's Background

Milgram had intended to investigate the importance of conformity among Germans, feeling that the influence of peers from that country might explain why so many people there violated their morals: "I plan to undertake a long series of experiments on obedience. While this series will stand by itself as an independent study, it is also preparation for the project on German character—in which comparative experimental measures of 'obedience to authority' will play an important part."[4]

An authority sets the goals, accepts responsibility, and determines what is ethical. Milgram pointed to the operation of the Nazi death camps, like Auschwitz, where millions of civilians were murdered: "The man at the concentration camp who actually dropped Cyclon B* into the gas chambers was able to justify *his* behavior on the ground that he was only following orders from above."[5]

Indeed, in the trials for war crimes following World War II, many Nazi officials insisted they were not personally guilty of war crimes "by claiming that they were only obeying orders."[6]

After completing his experiments, Milgram concluded, "Obedience is the psychological mechanism that links individual action to political purpose. It is the dispositional cement that binds men to systems of authority. Facts of recent history and observation in daily life suggest that for many people obedience may be a deeply ingrained behavior tendency, indeed, a prepotent [especially strong] impulse overriding training in ethics, sympathy, and moral conduct."[7]

The Turkish American social psychologist Muzafer Sherif* conducted research demonstrating that competition for limited resources increases prejudice toward members of out-groups* (out-groups are any group to which an individual does not belong). He found it also increases in-group* solidarity (the in-group being the one to which an individual belongs), and aggression toward out-group members.[8] This provided a persuasive parallel for the actions and thinking of non-Jewish Germans during the time leading up to the Holocaust.

For Germany, recovery from defeat in World War I* (1914–18), notably the profound economic depression that followed, created a feeling of helplessness. Jewish and non-Jewish Germans alike were competing for limited resources. In this case, the in-group consisted of non-Jewish Germans and the out-group of Jews. Therefore, destroying the out-group would make scarce resources more available for the in-group.

In their studies on conformity,[9] Sherif and the similarly influential social psychologist Solomon Asch* found that people often go along with the judgments of their peers, even when they know the judgments are wrong. This could help account for the actions of thousands of non-Nazis who tortured and killed Jews even when they knew that such actions were immoral.

NOTES

1   Stanley Milgram, *Obedience to Authority: An Experimental View* (New York: Harper & Row, 1974), 113.

2   Milgram, *Obedience to Authority*, 113.

3   Milgram, *Obedience to Authority*, 1.

4   Millgram, "Letter to Gordon Allport," October 10, 1960, Stanley Milgram Papers, Manuscripts and Archives, Yale University Library.

5   Milgram, *Obedience to Authority*, 11.

6   Ludy T. Benjamin, Jr. and Jeffrey A. Simpson, "The Power of the Situation: The Impact of Milgram's Obedience Studies on Personality and Social Psychology," *American Psychologist* 64, no. 1 (2009): 12–19.

7   Milgram, *Obedience to Authority*, 1.

8   Muzafer Sherif, O. Harvey, B. White, W. Hood, and C. Sherif, *Intergroup Conflict and Cooperation: The Robbers Cave Experiment* (Norman: Institute of Group Relations, University of Oklahoma, 1961).

9   Muzafer Sherif, "A Study of Some Social Factors in Perception," *Archives of Psychology* 27, no. 187 (1935): 1-60; and Solomon E. Asch, "Studies of Independence and Conformity: I. A Minority of One against a Unanimous Majority," *Psychological Monographs: General and Applied* 70, no. 9 (1956): 1–70.

MODULE 2
ACADEMIC CONTEXT

KEY POINTS

- Psychologists* during the 1930s, 1940s, and 1950s investigated different aspects of human behavior in an attempt to explain how totalitarian* governments (governments that control the citizen's life to an intrusive degree) hold on to power by exploiting human irrationality.

- Most of these investigators came from the field of social psychology*—the study of the ways in which people act in groups and how their individual behavior can be influenced by those around them.

- Psychologists investigated a cluster of traits, such as rigid adherence to rules, intolerance of weakness, and admiration for those in power, known as the "authoritarian personality,"* believing it to typify Germans, and Nazis* in particular.

The Work in its Context

Stanley Milgram's *Obedience to Authority: An Experimental View* is generally considered to fall within the "situationist" school of thought in the field of psychology.[1] Milgram believed that individuals' social situation, much more than their personality, plays the major role in determining behavior at any particular time.

"Personality psychologists," on the other hand, consider an individual's personality to be the most important predictor of their behavior. More recently, most psychologists agree that in reality there is an interaction between personality and situation. This "interactionist" approach is often viewed as a synthesis of the personality and situationist perspectives.

> 66 Most social acts have to be understood in their setting, and lose meaning if isolated. No error in thinking about social facts is more serious than the failure to see their place and function. 99
>
> Solomon Asch, *Social Psychology*

Milgram's work added significantly to our knowledge about conformity* and obedience. Milgram contributed to the ongoing growth in psychology's understanding of how individuals respond to pressure from other people. Particularly interested in social hierarchies (the ways in which societies are structured according to status), he demonstrated how effective commands can be if they are delivered by someone of higher rank. Milgram's most important finding was that the influence of a person who is seen as a legitimate authority can override an individual's own morals or ethics.

Ultimately, his findings supported the "interactionist" position of earlier psychologists who believed that behavior results from an interaction between the individual's personality and their situation. Interestingly, Milgram found that Roman Catholics* were more obedient than Jewish people and Protestants,* and that the more authoritarian the volunteers' personalities, the more closely they followed orders to inflict pain on others. ("Roman Catholic" and "Protestant" here refer to the major branches of the Christian faith; they differ in points of ritual and over the meaning of certain concepts related to Christian thought.)[2]

Overview of the Field

Milgram considered certain social scientists to be particularly important to the development of the field. "The contributions of [the social scientist and political philosopher Theodor] Adorno* ... and of [the German American political theorist] Hannah Arendt,* [the German social psychologist] Eric Fromm,* and [the foundational social scientist] Max Weber* are part of the zeitgeist* in which social scientists grow up," he wrote[3]—"zeitgeist" here meaning "the spirit of the times," in the sense of the wider social and intellectual context.

With the exception of Max Weber, who was born in 1864, these researchers came of age in the first half of the twentieth century: the period when fascism* took hold in Germany and Italy, leading to World War II.* They focused on personality traits and developed the "F scale"—a fascism test—that was designed to measure someone's readiness to accept a system of government in which a strong leader or dictator maintained total control while forcibly suppressing all criticism of his rule.

Fascism is an extreme right-wing system of government in which individuals are expected to put the interests of the state above their own. This system was in place in Italy from 1922 to 1943, and in Germany, where it was led by the Nazi Party,* from 1933 to 1945. The fascism test's authors—Adorno and his associates, the social scientists Else Frenkel-Brunswik,* Daniel Levinson,* and Nevitt Sanford*— found that people who scored high on this scale held negative, stereotyped attitudes toward members of any groups other than their own.[4] They came from homes where discipline was severe and threatening, causing a sense of powerlessness in the children. Hostility toward their parents was seething underneath overly respectful and obedient behavior. On the surface, such children adored their parents; underneath, they hated them.

Authoritarian personalities overvalue authority, while unconsciously despising it. When they grow up, such people feel an intense need to seek power and to identify with powerful people. Authoritarians are often unwilling to recognize or accept nuanced positions in politics or people. For example, they tend to believe that someone is all good or all bad, all superior or all inferior, rather than accepting that each person has a variety of strengths and weaknesses. Authoritarian personalities tend to harbor intense anger while not being conscious of it; they are not tolerant of weakness in themselves or others. Cruelty, selfishness, and hardness are seen as part of superiority. Kindness, sympathy, and generosity are believed to indicate weakness and inferiority.

These researchers believed that Germans typically had authoritarian personalities, because their society was patriarchal (founded on principles of male authority) with very strict child-rearing practices in which obedience to rules was central. They felt that this helped explain the deep hostility toward Jewish people, paranoia, and aggression that drove the Holocaust.*

Academic Influences

Milgram entered psychology when research about the dynamics of group behavior was being explored by the German American psychologist Kurt Lewin.*[5] Lewin believed that behavior at any moment was the result of interaction between the influence of other people, how the individual defined the situation, and rules that the individual had learned about how to behave with others. Milgram found this understanding very persuasive.

At around the same time, important work on prejudice was being done by Gordon Allport,* an American psychologist noted for his research into personality. Milgram was inspired by a chapter in Allport's book *The Nature of Prejudice* (1954), which identified stereotypes of different national characters.[6]

Milgram was also impressed by a key study carried out by Turkish American Muzafer Sherif.* This demonstrated the extent to which individuals can be influenced by opinions of other people when determining how much a pinpoint of light seemed to move when it was the only sight available in a dark room.[7]

Milgram worked as an assistant to the American social psychologist Solomon Asch* at Princeton University, and was impressed with Asch's work on conformity to peer pressure.*[8] He adapted Asch's methods when he went to Europe and undertook his own doctoral research, attempting to identify, measure, and compare the kinds of conformity typical of different nationalities. Instead of using Asch's method, in which participants judged the lengths of lines while hearing conflicting estimates from the people around them, he asked his participants to identify tones of sound. Like Asch, Milgram presented naive participants with the false perceptions of others to observe how much influence was exerted by peers.

Milgram was aware of a study by the American legal scholar Jerome Frank* that showed how an experimenter had persuaded participants to eat large quantities of salted crackers.[9] He was also familiar with work by John French* and Bertram Raven, psychologists noted for their research on social power, as well as others who considered the effects of authority in terms of legitimacy, the ability to bestow rewards, and coercion.[10]

NOTES

1   Solomon Asch, *Social Psychology* (Englewood Cliffs, NJ: Prentice-Hall, 1964), 2.

2   Stanley Milgram, "Group Pressure and Action Against a Person," *Journal of Abnormal and Social Psychology* 69, no. 2 (1964): 137–43.

3   Stanley Milgram, *Obedience to Authority: An Experimental View* (New York: Harper & Row, 1974), xiv.

4   Theodor Adorno, Else Frenkel-Brunswik, Daniel. J. Levinson, and R. Nevitt Sanford. *The Authoritarian Personality* (New York: Harper, 1950).

5   Kurt Lewin, *Field Theory in Social Science* (New York: Harper & Row, 1951).

6   Gordon W. Allport, *The Nature of Prejudice* (Reading, MA: Addison-Wesley, 1954).

7   Muzafer Sherif, "A Study of Some Social Factors in Perception," *Archives of Psychology* 27, no. 187 (1935): 1–60.

8   Solomon E. Asch, "Studies of Independence and Conformity: I. A Minority of One against a Unanimous Majority," *Psychological Monographs: General and Applied* 70, no. 9 (1956): 1–70.

9   Jerome Frank, "Experimental Studies of Personal Pressure and
     Resistance," *Journal of Genetic Psychology* 30 (1944): 23–64.

10   J. R. P. French and B. H. Raven, "The Bases of Social Power," in *Studies in
     Social Power*, ed. D. Cartwright (Ann Arbor: University of Michigan Press,
     1959), 150–67; R. Bierstedt, "The Problem of Authority," in *Freedom and
     Control in Modern Society*, ed. M. Berber et al. (New York: Van Nostrand,
     1954), 67–81; Arthur Koestler, *The Ghost in the Machine* (New York:
     Macmillan, 1967); and Alex Comfort, *Authority and Delinquency in the
     Modern State: A Criminological Approach to the Problem of Power* (London:
     Routledge and Kegan Paul, 1950).

MODULE 3
THE PROBLEM

KEY POINTS

- A central goal of Milgram's experiments was to examine the factors that lead an individual to obey—or disobey—orders from an authority, especially when the orders go against that individual's morals.

- The Nazi* leader Adolf Hitler* intended to depopulate Europe and relocate Jews to western Siberia; after meeting unexpected resistance to his invasion of Russia, he decided to kill them instead.

- Because Milgram heard that Nazi collaborators in the genocide of the Jews were "only following orders," he devised experiments to learn the extent to which ordinary people will obey orders to harm a stranger.

Core Question

Most importantly, Stanley Milgram's *Obedience to Authority: An Experimental View* examines those factors that make obedience and disobedience to authority more likely.

Milgram was motivated to conduct these studies by a desire to understand how the atrocities of the Holocaust* could have been carried out by people who claimed that they were simply following their superiors' orders. He points out that this type of claim has been made throughout history; he even cites cases in which American soldiers killed large number of civilians, apparently because they were following orders.[1]

These examples lead Milgram to claim that the tendency to obey an authority figure is a basic aspect of human nature. He goes on to argue that obedience to authority is encouraged and reinforced

> ❝ Fully appreciating the implications of these studies reduces the surprise experienced on learning that most of the low-level perpetrators of the Holocaust were ordinary people who lived unexceptional lives before and after their infamous deeds rather than self-selected psychopaths and sadists. ❞
>
> L. Ross, M. Lepper, and A. Ward, "History of Social Psychology: Insights, Challenges, and Contributions to Theory and Application"

through early socialization—the training children receive at home, in school, and so on, in how to live with other people. Furthermore, he argues that concepts such as loyalty directly relate to the tendency to obey authority figures, and are often celebrated as virtues in our society.[2] Indeed, social living requires, to some degree, that individuals are willing to do as they are told. Sadly, as in the case of the Holocaust, the outcomes of such obedience depend in part on the degree to which the authority figures place value on the lives of everyone in society.

The Participants

When Adolf Hitler was a young man in Vienna, he noticed that politicians' power increased when they exploited anti-Semitism* (hatred of Jews). He also became attracted to writings by the sixteenth-century religious scholar Martin Luther,* a key figure in the schism in the European Church that led to the split between the Roman Catholic* and Protestant* branches of Christianity. Luther recommended that Germans burn all synagogues, force Jews to do physical labor, and expel them from provinces where Christians lived.[3]

Following Luther, Hitler used anti-Semitism to build in-group* solidarity. In 1938, in an event that came to be known as "The Night of Broken Glass," Hitler's forces destroyed most of Germany's synagogues and murdered dozens of Jews. Eventually, the Nazis rounded up and killed almost all German Jews, using some for slave labor first. The historian Daniel Goldhagen* has argued that this radical strain of anti-Semitism in Germany helped explain the Holocaust.[4] It should be noted, however, that anti-Semitism was more intense in Romania, Estonia, Poland, Austria, and Russia than in Germany, and that massacres of Jews had been perpetrated by Russians for many years—and yet this never led to the type of mass killings carried out by Hitler.[5]

A central goal for Hitler was to "make room" in Europe for the German people. In many ways, this was similar to the manner in which European settlers had gradually taken over most of North America and resettled the Native Americans onto small "reservations" in less desirable regions. Hitler initially intended to make room by relocating huge numbers of Eastern Europe's residents—not just the Jews—to western Siberia, or else by simply starving them to death. As the historian Omer Bartov put it, "The ideal war, according to Hitler, was one of conquest, subjugation, and extermination."[6]

Hitler had planned to occupy and depopulate Russia, which would have allowed much more space for relocating Jews. But while his invasion killed millions of Russians, German armies encountered unexpected resistance during 1941; it was in light of this that Hitler switched his strategy from relocating Jews to Siberia, Madagascar, and Palestine, to eliminating them entirely.

In 1942, Hitler told the members of the Nazi party, "Today … my prophecy shall hold true that it is not the Aryan race that will be destroyed in this war, but rather it is the Jew who will be exterminated … And only then, after the elimination of these parasites, will a long period of international understanding and thus true peace spread over the suffering world."[7]

"Such statements," the historian Omer Bartov wrote, "were greeted in Germany not with [calm acceptance], but with enthusiasm … In order to understand the origins of the Holocaust, we must understand the origins of this public attitude in Germany. It was a combination of technocratic activism [the ability and willingness to carry out mass murder on an industrial scale] and public complicity that made the great crime possible, and the former would not have accomplished much without the latter."[8]

On July 16, 1941, Rolf-Heinz Hoeppner, a Nazi official charged with "resettlement affairs" in Poznan, Poland, wrote a memorandum to his boss, Adolf Eichmann,* a man who played a significant role in the logistics of the industrialized mass murder of Jewish people: "There is a danger that, in the coming winter, it will become impossible to feed all the Jews. It must seriously be considered whether the most humane solution is to finish off the Jews unfit for labor through some fast-acting means."[9]

The Contemporary Debate

Carrying out a policy "to finish off the Jews" involved ordinary people, not just Nazis. The murder of about six million Jewish people involved approximately 200,000 collaborators. "The consensus in German scholarship and public opinion," writes Bertov, "was that discipline, authority, and peer group pressure had played a much greater role than anti-Semitism and ideological motivation."[10]

To understand how ordinary men are transformed into mass murderers by pressure of authority, Stanley Milgram ran a series of experiments. He found that volunteers obeyed an instructor's directions to continue administering shocks at higher and higher intensities even when this could have lethal consequences. Milgram wrote that "The essence of obedience consists in the fact that a person comes to view himself as the instrument for carrying out another person's wishes, and he therefore no longer regards himself as responsible for his actions. Once this crucial shift of viewpoint has occurred in the person, all of the essential features of obedience follow."[11]

In the book's introduction, he makes some important points regarding obedience and authority:

- "Obedience is the psychological mechanism that links individual action to political purpose."[12]
- "It is the extreme willingness of adults to go to almost any length on the command of an authority that constitutes the chief finding of the study."[13]
- "The Nazi extermination of European Jews is the most extreme instance of abhorrent immoral acts carried out by thousands of people in the name of obedience."[14]
- "Ordinary people, simply doing their jobs, without any particular hostility on their part, can become agents in a terrible destructive process."[15]

Milgram further considered the similarities between those who carried out the Holocaust and the volunteers in his obedience experiments: "While many of the people studied in the experiment were in some sense against what they did to the learner, and many protested even while they obeyed … what they lacked was the capacity for transforming beliefs and values into action. Some were totally convinced of the wrongness of what they were doing but could not bring themselves to make an open break with authority."[16]

Paralleling this finding with the Holocaust, Milgram wrote that the "attitudes of the guards at a concentration camp are of no consequence when in fact they are allowing the slaughter of innocent men to take place before them."[17]

In applying his experiment's findings to the Holocaust, Milgram conceded that "at least one essential feature of the situation in Germany was not studied here—namely, the intense devaluation of the victim prior to action against him … [In] all likelihood, our subjects would have experienced greater ease in shocking the victim had he been convincingly portrayed as a brutal criminal or a pervert."[18]

Milgram adds that in "the final analysis, what happened in Germany from 1933 to 1945 can only be fully understood as the expression of a unique historical development that will never again be precisely replicated."[19]

NOTES

1   Stanley Milgram, *Obedience to Authority: An Experimental View* (New York: Harper & Row, 1974), 179–89.

2   Milgram, *Obedience to Authority*, 139–52.

3   Martin Luther, "Concerning Jews and Their Lies," in *The Jew in the Medieval World*, ed. Jacob Marcus (New York: Harper Row, 1965), 167–9.

4   Daniel J. Goldhagen, *Hitler's Willing Executioners: Ordinary Germans and the Holocaust* (New York: Little, Brown, 1996).

5   Franklin H. Littell, *Hyping the Holocaust: Scholars Answer Goldhagen* (Merion Station, PA: Merion Westfield Press, 1997).

6   Omer Bartov, *Germany's War and the Holocaust: Disputed Histories* (Ithaca, NY: Cornell University Press, 2003), 4.

7   Bartov, Germany's War, 98.

8   Bartov, Germany's War, 98.

9   Bartov, Germany's War, 94.

10 Bartov, Germany's War, 157.

11 Milgram, *Obedience to Authority*, XII.

12 Milgram, *Obedience to Authority*, 1.

13 Milgram, *Obedience to Authority*, 5.

14 Milgram, *Obedience to Authority*, 2.

15 Milgram, *Obedience to Authority*, 5–6.

16 Milgram, *Obedience to Authority*, 9.

17 Milgram, *Obedience to Authority*, 9–10.

18 Milgram, *Obedience to Authority*, 9–10.

19 Milgram, *Obedience to Authority*, 177.

MODULE 4
THE AUTHOR'S CONTRIBUTION

KEY POINTS

- Psychological* tests on high-level Nazi* officials showed they were not psychopaths (people whose social behavior is fundamentally damaged, and who are incapable of empathy) but relatively well adjusted; Milgram devised experiments to see if other "normal" individuals could be brought, by obedience to authority, to commit immoral acts.

- The more remote perpetrators are from victims, the more severe the damage they are willing to do.

- People are more likely to obey their conscience and defy an evil authority if they are not alone, but joined by an ally.

Author's Aims

The experiments that Stanley Milgram reports in *Obedience to Authority: An Experimental View* sought to subject the study of obedience to a controlled scientific process.

He knew that psychological examinations of several top Nazi officials captured after World War II* had shown them to be "normal." In their defense during trials for crimes against humanity, these men had pleaded that they were just following orders. Milgram hoped that his studies' results could help explain how Germans who were not vicious psychopaths (that is, criminally insane) could obey orders to systematically murder six million Jews. To this end, Milgram posited, "It is psychologically easy to ignore responsibility when one is only an intermediate link in a chain of evil action but is far from the final consequences of the action."[1]

> ❝ People understand that soldiers massacre, but they fail to see that an action such as this, routinely carried out, is the logical outcome of processes that are at work in less visible form throughout organized society. ❞
>
> Stanley Milgram, *Obedience to Authority: An Experimental View*

If it were true that Nazi collaborators permitted themselves to perform unconscionable acts because they were merely following orders, then, Milgram thought, it should be possible to reproduce this situation in a psychology lab. He intended to refine his experimental procedures in the United States before going to Europe and running the same experiment on Germans for comparison. This would help reveal whether such unusual levels of obedience were part of the national German character. He also devised experiments to test conformity* to peer pressure,* given that this tendency relates to obedience.

Approach

"To study obedience most simply," Milgram wrote, "we must create a situation in which one person orders another person to perform an observable action and we must note when obedience to the imperative occurs and when it fails."[2]

By deceiving volunteers into thinking that they were participating in a study about the effects of punishment on memory, Milgram devised a situation in which ordinary adults were asked to inflict severe—possibly lethal—pain on fellow human beings. By obeying such orders, his volunteers would reveal the extent to which ordinary people will obey an authority when it means hurting a stranger. Participants in the Holocaust were obeying the authority of Germany's Nazi government; the experiment's counterpart was the scientific authority of the experimenter, who was introduced as a research psychologist. This, in turn, was designed to cast light on whether the war criminals committed atrocities simply because of their readiness to follow orders, and not necessarily because they hated the Jews.

Milgram's volunteers were led into giving what appeared to be near-lethal levels of electric shock by a series of gradually increasing steps. The authority came in the form of an emotionless, lab-coated experimenter who demanded that they deliver shocks of greater intensity for each mistake made by a "learner" (who was in reality working for Milgram and not actually receiving any shocks).

Milgram generated 19 variations of the experiment. The greatest compliance with the demand to administer the highest intensity shocks occurred when the "learner" was sitting in a different room from the volunteer, who could nonetheless hear the former's yelps and protests.

Contribution in Context

The results of Milgram's experiments were stunning. Between 30 and 65 percent of his volunteers fully obeyed the experimenter and delivered the maximum intensity of shock, even when the "learner" repeatedly protested, "Let me out of here. I have a heart condition." Many volunteers persisted in raising the intensity of shocks even after the "learner" stopped responding, interpreting the lack of response as a wrong answer. The silence could have led the volunteer to conclude that the "learner" had become unconscious, or had even died; and yet the shocks were continued.

Across the variations in the experiment, fewer volunteers administered the maximum shock voltage when they could see the "victim" than when the latter was in another room and could only be heard. Also, fewer volunteers administered the maximum voltage when they were required to hold the victim's hand on a metal plate to do so. Such findings paralleled situations in which high-level Nazi officials gave orders from afar, rather than killing people with their own hands and directly witnessing the suffering they were causing.

The maximum voltage that the volunteer administered was far less when a peer—a fellow volunteer—was in the same room, and when both the volunteer and the peer could ask the experimenter's permission to stop the procedure. This observation suggests that conscientious objectors have a greater potential for stopping a country from going to war as their numbers increase.

Subjects were less obedient when the authority figure was played by someone other than the impassive, lab-coated individual. This shows that status has an important effect on the extent of influence held by an authority figure—and the likelihood of their being defied.

Milgram's contribution was significant. He may have uncovered an aspect of human nature that contributed to the extraordinarily awful, murderous acts of Germans under the control of the Nazis during World War II. His findings offered both an explanation and a warning.

NOTES

1   Stanley Milgram, *Obedience to Authority: An Experimental View* (New York: Harper & Row, 1974), 11.

2   Milgram, *Obedience to Authority*, 13.

SECTION 2
IDEAS

MODULE 5
MAIN IDEAS

KEY POINTS

- Milgram identified several factors that make obedience more likely: binding factors* (factors that maintain the stability of the social hierarchy), agentic shift* (handing over responsibility for actions to an authority figure), and counter-anthropomorphism* (the tendency not to recognize human influence in the operation of political and social institutions).

- Milgram believed that obedient subjects see themselves not as people acting in a morally accountable way, but as the agents of external authority.

- The book is written in a clear, down-to-earth way, and provides ample quotes from interviews with participants in his experiments, giving the reader a better sense of how they felt and why they remained obedient even when it meant hurting another person.

Key Themes

Stanley Milgram's 1974 book *Obedience to Authority: An Experimental View* aimed, above all, to identify those factors that make obedience to authority most likely to occur, even when it results in behavior that the individual finds morally wrong. Striving to understand how people can engage in behavior that they feel is immoral simply because they are obeying orders, Milgram was also interested in the factors that make disobedience more likely.

While introducing a theoretical framework, Milgram focuses on several factors as being especially important for understanding how presumably good people can "lend themselves to the purposes of authority and become instruments in its destructive processes."[1]

> ❝ Tyrannies are perpetuated by diffident men who do not possess the courage to act out their beliefs. ❞
>
> Stanley Milgram, *Obedience to Authority: An Experimental View*

Broadly speaking, Milgram identified *binding factors*, an *agentic shift*, and *counter-anthropomorphism* as key issues in determining whether an individual obeys or disobeys an authority figure.[2]

Exploring the Ideas

According to Milgram, binding factors make it less likely that an individual will leave a situation in which obedience is requested. These factors can arise from both within and outside an individual. For instance, Milgram cites the participant's "politeness, his initial promise of aid to the experimenter, and the awkwardness of withdrawal"[3] as potential binding factors for the participants in the experiments described in the book.

Another key to understanding participants' continued obedience is their sense of who is responsible for their actions. Here, Milgram argues that the participants experience an agentic shift: in the context of his experiments, they attributed responsibility for their actions to the experimenter—the authority figure. Indeed, Milgram states that the participant saw himself "as not responsible for his own actions … attributing all initiative to the experimenter, a legitimate authority … He sees himself not as the agent of external authority."[4]

Finally, Milgram argues that viewing the authority as a part of an institution promotes obedience. In other words, an individual is more willing to obey orders that come through an institutional structure, because this somehow transcends the human element. In fact, Milgram indicates that "some people treat systems of human origin as if they existed above and beyond any human agent." This tendency is called counter-anthropomorphism. "Thus when the experimenter says,

'This experiment requires that you continue,' the subject feels this to be an imperative that goes beyond any merely human command.'"[5]

Language and Expression

Milgram's *Obedience to Authority* quotes extensively from papers that he had already published in scientific journals, so the book might be expected to be full of technical jargon that could be problematic for the average reader. But in fact it is written in the clearest possible language; no technical knowledge is required to understand it. As long as the reader has at least a passing familiarity with some of the other major figures and movements in the history of psychology* (Sigmund Freud,* for example, who pioneered the theoretical and therapeutic method of psychoanalysis,* founded on the principle that our thought and behavior are affected by the unconscious mind), the comparisons that Milgram makes across various areas of the discipline are easy to follow.

The organization of chapters and sub-chapters is logical and elegantly structured. For the greater part of the book, the reader is offered concrete examples of the series of experiments that Milgram conducted. Several chapters provide excerpts from interviews with research participants. Together, these give the reader a true grasp not only of what the participants did, but of what they said and thought about their experiences. Even the book's closing chapters, in which Milgram shifts from the concrete to the theoretical, are written in a way that is easily accessible to readers.

NOTES

1   Stanley Milgram, *Obedience to Authority: An Experimental View* (New York: Harper & Row, 1974), 180.

2   Milgram, *Obedience to Authority*, 1–12.

3   Milgram, *Obedience to Authority,* 7.

4   Milgram, *Obedience to Authority,* 7–8.

5   Milgram, *Obedience to Authority,* 8–9.

MODULE 6
SECONDARY IDEAS

KEY POINTS

- Milgram showed that obedience to authority is influenced by the nature and position of the authority, the position of the victim, and the social setting in which obedience occurs.

- Manipulating these variables can have a significant impact on the likelihood of obedience.

- In response to criticism, Milgram conceded that his findings gave only a partial understanding of those who carried out the Holocaust.

Other Ideas

The secondary themes of Stanley Milgram's *Obedience to Authority: An Experimental View* involve the specific variables explored in the experiments described; there were 19 versions of the experiment, each designed to consider slightly different factors. Specifically, Milgram found that the nature and proximity of the authority figure, the closeness of the victim (or learner in this context), and the social setting in which participants found themselves were all especially important considerations.

In some of his studies, Milgram varied the location of the authority figure and the way in which he or she interacted with the research participant. For instance, early versions of the study involved the authority figure wearing a gray lab coat, sitting in the same room and speaking directly to the participant. Later versions, however, had the experimenter in another room, providing instructions to the participant by means of telephone.

> ❝ Authority systems must be based on people arranged in a hierarchy ... Obedience to authority occurs within a hierarchical structure in which the actor feels that the person above has the right to prescribe behavior. Conformity regulates the behavior among those of equal status; obedience links one status to another. ❞
>
> Stanley Milgram, *Obedience to Authority: An Experimental View*

Milgram also had an ingenious way of manipulating the nature of the authority figure. In some circumstances, the experimenter would be called away for some important task, and someone else, believed by the participant to be another research volunteer, would take over the role. In this way, Milgram manipulated the legitimacy of the authority in the eyes of the participant.

Milgram also varied the location of the victim, and the nature of the interaction between the participant and the victim. For most of the studies, the victim was strapped to a chair in a different room, and audio recordings of the victim's protests were played. At other times, the victim was moved into the room with the participant, and in some cases, the participant had to physically place the victim's hand onto an electric shock plate to administer the punishment.

Finally, the research participant was sometimes in a room with several others who pretended to be participants as well. In some of these studies, the other participants would model disobedience. In this variation, Milgram was looking to understand how the presence and behavior of others would affect the behavior of the participants.

Exploring the Ideas

After varying the closeness of the victim, the proximity of the authority figure, and the social context, Milgram made several interesting observations. When the authority figure was at a distance, levels of obedience dropped dramatically; furthermore, participants would sometimes administer "lower shocks than were required and never informed the experimenter of their deviation from the correct procedure."[1] Some participants refused to continue when communicating with the experimenter over the phone. They became obedient again, however, if the latter returned to the room to give instructions directly.

Milgram concludes that the research participants "seemed able to resist the experimenter far better when they did not have to confront him face to face."[2]

One of the most significant findings in the obedience experiments is that the greatest obedience and most intense shocks were delivered when the research participant was the greatest distance from the victim. Generalizing these findings to situations outside the psychology* laboratory, Milgram said that people generally "do not directly carry out any destructive actions. They shuffle papers or load ammunition or perform some other act which, though it contributes to the final destructive effect, is remote from it in the eyes and mind of the functionary."[3]

Another interesting finding emerged when Milgram varied the social setting for the research. In some of the studies, other individuals who appeared to be fellow participants (in fact actors working for Milgram) would act out disobedience by refusing to continue with the study. Once again, Milgram observed that rates of obedience dropped significantly at these times. He indicates that of all the various manipulations "none was so effective at undercutting the experimenter's authority as the manipulation reported here."[4]

Overlooked

In attacking Milgram's conclusions, his critics often addressed issues that the author had already recognized and answered in *Obedience to Authority*. Their objections and accusations were frequently based only on their readings of his earliest reports, not on his comprehensive accounts or on the reflections that made up the 1974 publication.

One such objection was that the results of his obedience experiments provide only limited insight into those who carried out the Holocaust.*[5] But Milgram had already conceded precisely that point; while it was true that he had at first exaggerated the extent to which his findings could be applied to the aggression that was unleashed on European Jews from 1933 to 1945, he had softened his position by the time he wrote his reflections in the book.

Some commentators emphasized the high defiance rate observed when the instructor was not a lab-coated, impassive technician.[6] They considered this to undermine Milgram's interpretations. Yet Milgram addressed such effects in his discussion of hierarchical organization in social structures; he suggested that, far from undermining his conclusions, these results strengthened them, arguing that "orders originating outside of authority lose all force."[7]

NOTES

1   Stanley Milgram, *Obedience to Authority: An Experimental View* (New York: Harper & Row, 1974), 62.

2   Milgram, *Obedience to Authority,* 62.

3   Milgram, *Obedience to Authority,* 121

4   Milgram, *Obedience to Authority,* 118.

5   Charles Helm and Mario Morelli, "Obedience to Authority in a Laboratory Setting: Generalizability and Context Dependency," *Political Studies* 33 (1985): 610–27.

6   J. M. Burger. "Situational Variables in Milgram's Experiment That Kept His Participants Shocking," *Journal of Social Issues* 70 (2014): 489–500.

7   Milgram, *Obedience to Authority,* 104.

MODULE 7
ACHIEVEMENT

KEY POINTS

- Milgram demonstrated the extent to which people obey authorities even when the commanded actions conflict with their personal morals.

- For Milgram, the massacre of 347 civilians by American soldiers in the village of My Lai* during the Vietnam War* was another example of people's tendency to obey authority even when ordered to carry out awful acts.

- Milgram stressed that those who commit evil acts under orders are often not motivated by aggression, merely by obedience.

Assessing the Argument

Stanley Milgram wrote *Obedience to Authority: An Experimental View,* and designed the experiments described in the book, to try to understand the political and historical events that had taken place in Europe during World War II*—then only two decades earlier. "It is only logical that a philosophy of government that has human inequality as its touchstone will also elevate obedience as an absolute virtue … It is no accident that the hallmark of [Nazi* Germany] was its emphasis both on the concept of superior and inferior groups and on quick, impressive, and prideful obedience, with clicking boots and the ready execution of command."[1]

Milgram created a laboratory model for obedience and the hierarchy of social roles. Building on accounts given by the social psychologists* who came before him, he made a useful contribution

> **❝** Obedience arises out of and perpetuates inequalities in human relationships and thus, in its ultimate expression, is the ideal regulatory mechanism of fascism. **❞**
>
> Stanley Milgram, *Obedience to Authority: An Experimental View*.

to explanations for the murderous acts that Germans carried out against their fellow citizens.

The most important factor in Milgram's achievement was the ingenious design of his experiments. The interpretations that he offered for the results went beyond any political point of view; rather, they identified aspects of human nature. Similar results were obtained when his procedures were repeated in other countries such as Australia, Germany, Italy, and South Africa,[2] suggesting that they represent a universal phenomenon.

If it were true that Nazi officials were merely following orders, then Milgram thought that the level of obedience they showed was extraordinary because their acts went deeply against common ethics. When he tried to recreate a somewhat parallel situation with his experiments in America, the results he obtained were so stunning that he recognized that obedience to authority was much more common than had been believed.

Additionally, Milgram found that the most obedient participants had authoritarian personalities,* and that Roman Catholic* Christians were less defiant than Protestant* Christians and Jews. This shed light on the personalities and social categories, in terms of population, of those who perpetrated the Holocaust.*[3] The findings also provided support for social psychologist Kurt Lewin's* model of behavior as an interaction between the forces of personality and those of the situation in which people find themselves.[4]

Achievement in Context

It is important to recognize that Milgram's book was published in 1974, just as the Vietnam War was coming to a close. During this war, American soldiers were found to have been involved in massacres of civilians. The best-known case was the massacre of 347 civilians in the South Vietnamese village of My Lai in 1968. Milgram's book drew parallels between these atrocities and those of the Nazis. He cites an interview with one of the American soldiers who had participated, in which he claimed to have been "just following orders"[5]—exactly as scores of Nazi officers had done at the Nuremberg Trials,* where people were tried for crimes against humanity following World War II.* Additionally, Milgram was astonished to find that more than half of Americans believed that William Calley,* the officer responsible for the My Lai massacre, should not be punished for his actions.[6]

The fact that Americans were just as capable as Nazis of violating common morality suggested that such obedience may be a basic aspect of human nature, and not unique to Germans. This finding resonated deeply among the American people, and Stanley Milgram soon became a household name.

Milgram's book had considerable impact on popular culture. For example, his experiments have been referenced in plays such as George Bellak's* *The Tenth Level* (1976), Dannie Abse's* *The Dogs of Pavlov* (1973), Anthony Cardinale's* *Tolliver's Trick* (1987), and in films such as *I as in Icarus* (1979), *Atrocity* (2005), and *Experimenter* (2015). The book informed novels such as Eileen Coughlan's* *Dying by Degrees* (2000) and music such as the British musician Peter Gabriel's* 1986 song "We Do What We're Told (Milgram's 37)."

The impact of *Obedience to Authority* has persisted long after its first publication in 1974; the studies that it describes have continued to be discussed in scholarly journals. According to Google Scholar, which tracks how often books and articles are referred to by other authors, it has been cited more than 7,500 times.[7]

Limitations

Although Milgram's experiments were inspired by an attempt to understand the horrific events of the Holocaust, he was well aware that his laboratory studies did not provide a perfect analogy for what had happened in Nazi Germany. They did, however, illustrate how obedience to authority is part of the workings of social hierarchy. To clarify his position, Milgram wrote, "Although aggressive tendencies are part and parcel of human nature, they have hardly anything to do with the behavior observed in the experiment … The act of shocking the victim does not stem from destructive urges but from the fact that subjects have become integrated into a social structure and are unable to get out of it."[8]

Indeed, when research participants were given the option to control the level of shock used as punishment they "administered the lowest shocks on the control panel."[9]

To further illustrate the difference between obedience and aggressive urges, Milgram provided the following example. "Suppose the experimenter instructed the subject to drink a glass of water. Does this mean the subject is thirsty? Obviously not, for he is simply doing what he is told to do. It is the essence of obedience that the action carried out does not correspond to the motives of the actor but is initiated in the motive system of those higher up in the social hierarchy."[10]

NOTES

1   Stanley Milgram, *Obedience to Authority: An Experimental View* (New York: Harper & Row, 1974), 207

2   Milgram, *Obedience to Authority*, 171.

3   Stanley Milgram, "Group Pressure and Action Against a Person," *Journal of Abnormal and Social Psychology* 69, no. 2 (1964): 137–43.

4   Kurt Lewin, *Field Theory in Social Science* (New York: Harper & Row, 1951).

5   Milgram, *Obedience to Authority*, 179–89.

6   Milgram, Obedience to Authority, 211; H. Kelman and L. Lawrence,
    "Assignment of Responsibility in the Case of Lt. Calley: Preliminary Report
    on a National Survey," *Journal of Social Issues* 28, no. 1 (1972): 177–212.

7   Google Scholar, "Obedience to Authority," accessed
    May 16, 2016, https://scholar.google.com/
    scholar?hl=en&q=Obedience+to+Authority+&btnG=&as_sdt=1%2C9&as_
    sdtp=.

8   Milgram, *Obedience to Authority,* 166.

9   Milgram, *Obedience to Authority,* 166.

10 Milgram, *Obedience to Authority,* 166.

MODULE 8
PLACE IN THE AUTHOR'S WORK

KEY POINTS

- Milgram's life's work was concerned with how people act in social situations.

- Milgram's obedience studies showed an "agentic shift,"* in which individuals shift responsibility for their actions to an authority.

- Milgram's reputation was based primarily upon his research on obedience to authority.

Positioning

Stanley Milgram's *Obedience to Authority: An Experimental View* was published in 1974, some time after his work on obedience had begun. In fact, large portions of the book were taken directly from articles that he had published in scientific journals years before. Prior to carrying out this work, Milgram was not a specialist within the field of social psychology.* All his studies dealt with how people interact with each other; much of his research examined how people treat strangers and how behavior is influenced by those around us.

Milgram's first works were concerned with levels of conformity* to peer pressure* among people of different nationalities.[1] His conformity studies were followed by 24 studies on obedience to authority.[2] Both these groups of studies were inspired by the author's puzzlement about those who carried out the Holocaust.*

Milgram only spent a few years studying the topic of obedience, along with a sabbatical that he spent writing summaries and responses to comments about his papers. He also published reports on the effects of violence seen on television,[3] and conducted experiments that

> **❝** While the existence of authority sometimes leads to the commission of ruthless and immoral acts, the absence of authority renders one a victim to such acts on the part of others who are better organized. Were the United States to abandon all forms of political authority we would soon become the victims of our own disorganization, because better organized societies would immediately perceive and act on the opportunities that weakness creates. **❞**
>
> Stanley Milgram, *Obedience to Authority: An Experimental View*

helped pioneer the field of urban psychology (the study of how the environment affects the psychology of urban dwellers). There he investigated:

- how likely people are to give up their seats to strangers on buses and subway trains
- how closely connected we are to people remotely located from us[4]
- how city dwellers create maps in their heads to orient themselves
- how the excessive stimulation of city life causes so much sensory and emotional overload that people tend to avoid eye contact with each other and communication with strangers.[5]

Integration

Milgram's research into obedience flowed from his studies on conformity: originally he had sought to identify levels of conformity to peer pressure and then look at obedience to authority, hoping to observe the extent to which these tendencies were present in the cultures of different nations. Several variations of his obedience experiment included the presence of peers (that is, members of the same social group). In some experiments, he observed the extent of obedience to authority as a function of conformity to peer opinion, intending to compare obedience levels in the United States to those in Germany.

Milgram believed that obedient participants had handed over responsibility for their harmful actions to the experimenter. He believed that participants only carried out such actions because it was a requirement of the experiment in which they had agreed to participate. Milgram termed this process "agentic shift"[6] because participants shifted "agency" (roughly, responsibility) for their actions to the experimenter. This idea was not universally accepted among social psychologists. Some claimed that participants knew that they themselves were harming the "learner," and regretted it.[7]

Some also cast doubt on the parallel between Milgram's experiments and the Holocaust,* because many of those who had actively carried out its atrocities had been devoted believers in the Nazi* view that the world would be better without the Jews.[8] So they did not need to employ such agentic shift in order to justify their actions. In *Obedience to Authority*, Milgram did not retract his belief in the agentic shift, but he conceded that an analogy between his experiments and the Holocaust was stretching the point: the likelihood that obedience would cause people to "harm" the victim in his experiments would have been greater if the victims were devalued, as Jews had been during the Holocaust.[9]

Significance

The obedience studies were the biggest accomplishment of Milgram's career, establishing his reputation. As one commentator puts it, "Milgram was also on solid ground in pinpointing obedience to authority as a possible key to understanding the Holocaust, given the high value placed on it by Nazi ideology and German culture generally. For example, the first of twelve commandments listed in a primer used to indoctrinate Nazi youth was 'The leader is always right.' And many generations of German children grew up on cautionary tales such as Shockheaded Peter.* The tale's moral was that disobedience could lead to rather drastic, violent consequences."[10]

To say that Milgram's work was significant would be an understatement; the importance of his work was swiftly recognized. In 1964, he was awarded the Socio-Psychological Prize from the American Association for the Advancement of Science. Further honors came later in his career when he was elected to the American Academy of Arts and Sciences in 1983, which provided "further testimony to the interdisciplinary scope of interest in his research."[11]

NOTES

1   Stanley Milgram, "Nationality and Conformity," *Scientific American* 205, no. 6 (1961): 45–51.

2   Stanley Milgram, "Behavioral Study of Obedience," *Journal of Abnormal and Social Psychology* 67 (1963): 371–8.

3   Stanley Milgram and R. L. Shotland, eds, *Television and Antisocial Behavior: Field Experiments* (New York: Academic Press, 1973).

4   Stanley Milgram, "The Small World Problem," *Psychology Today* 2 (1967): 60–67; Judith Kleinfeld, "Six Degrees of Separation: Urban Myth?" *Psychology Today* 35, no. 2 (March/April 2002): 74; and H. White, "Search for the Parameters of the Small World Phenomenon," *Social Forces* 49, no. 2 (1970): 259–64.

5   Stanley Milgram, *The Individual in a Social World: Essays and Experiments*, 2nd edn (New York: McGraw-Hill, 1992).

6   Bob M. Fennis and Henk Aarts, "Revisiting the Agentic Shift: Weakening Personal Control Increases Susceptibility to Social Influence," *European Journal of Social Psychology* 42, no 7 (2012): 824–31.

7   Diana Baumrind, "Some Thoughts on the Ethics of Research: After Reading Milgram's 'Behavioral Study of Obedience.'" *American Psychologist* 19, no. 6 (1964): 421–3.

8   George R. Mastroianni, "Milgram and the Holocaust: A Reexamination," *Journal of Theoretical and Philosophical Psychology* 22, no. 2 (2002): 158–

73.

9   Stanley Milgram, *Obedience to Authority: An Experimental View* (New York: Harper & Row, 1974), 176–7.

10 Thomas Blass, *The Man Who Shocked the World: The Life and Legacy of Stanley Milgram* (New York: Basic Books, 2004), 271.

11 Arthur G. Miller, *The Obedience Experiments: A Case Study of Controversy in Social Science* (New York: Praeger, 1986), 286.

SECTION 3
IMPACT

MODULE 9
THE FIRST RESPONSES

KEY POINTS

- Milgram conceded that his experiment results might not be entirely relevant to the Holocaust,* since his subjects did not have the goal of harming their victims—unlike those who helped carry out the crimes of humanity suffered by European Jews.

- Unlike the perpetrators of the Holocaust, Milgram's participants were concerned about their victims, and they trusted the experimenter's assurance that the shocks, though painful, would not cause any physical damage.

- Milgram at first thought his experiments showed that Americans could, under the right circumstances, be brought to act as the Germans who murdered Jews had done; he later pulled back from that conclusion.

Criticism

Stanley Milgram's *Obedience to Authority: An Experimental View* was not without its critics. In general, these lines of criticism fell into one of several themes. First, there was concern that the artificial nature of the laboratory could not provide significant insight into how obedience to authority plays out in the real world. There were also questions about the extent to which the experiment's participants represented the general population. Indeed, Milgram acknowledged his critics' arguments that "(1) the people studied in the experiment are not typical, (2) they didn't believe that they were administering shocks … and (3) it is not possible to generalize from the laboratory to the larger world."[1]

> ❝ Milgram recognized that meaningful social situations only make sense to the actors' because these interactions are structured according to norms and rules with which the participants are already familiar. He claimed that his social-psychological experiments on obedience had a normative structure that was embedded in the larger society's moral order. ❞
>
> Johannes Lang, "Against Obedience"

Psychologists* rejected the validity of Milgram's conclusions on several grounds. For a number of reasons, the results might not apply to the Germans who carried out the Holocaust (and, indeed, Milgram himself acknowledged most of these reasons in his book). Milgram's participants knew that they were in an experiment, not in a war-torn environment in desperate times. In fact, follow-up surveys revealed that about 20 percent of his volunteers were not deceived by the experiment's setting or instructions; they doubted that the actor who played the learner was actually receiving shocks. This indicates that some participants merely acted as though they believed in their task; their responses, then, were made to satisfy the experimenter, which might lower the actual levels of obedience observed.[2]

Another issue was that even volunteers who believed the deception did not decide to harm another person out of anger or hatred, but were helping a psychologist test the effectiveness of punishment on learning. The volunteers' motive for inflicting pain, then, was not comparable to those of Holocaust perpetrators. Those who were killing Jews considered their actions to be, in the words of sociologist Jack Katz,* "righteous slaughter"[3]—harming their victims was not an unfortunate by-product, but their primary goal.

Yet even on this issue, if the actions taken by most perpetrators of the Holocaust were performed more out of a sense of duty than hatred, paralleling the two groups can be seen as not especially problematic. Milgram felt that his participants acted out of a sense of obligation as subjects in an experiment, not from any aggressive tendencies. Both the Germans and Milgram's volunteers, then, were motivated by duty.

Responses

In response to criticism, Milgram stressed that violating morals out of obedience is made easier by handing responsibility to the authority giving the orders. He argued that entering this "agentic"* state of mind—shifting the decision to act to an authority figure—is not unpleasant; following instructions shelters an individual from the negative ethical consequences of their actions. It is the disobedient subject, then, and "not the obedient subject, who experiences the burden of his action."[4] Yet Milgram's claim was challenged by several facts: subjects were obviously distressed when they obeyed and continued to shock the learner, and often challenged the experimenter; furthermore, the degree of compliance varied across conditions. If Milgram's claims were true, it could be argued that the level of compliance should have been the same whether the subject was alone, for example, or with a friend.

Other important differences existed between Milgram's experiments and the Holocaust. First, most of Milgram's volunteers believed that they were working for the advancement of science, not on Nazi instructions to rid the world of Jews. Second, Milgram's lab-coated experimenter assured volunteers that, though painful, the shocks could not cause any physical damage. Third, the victim was a friendly, likeable man, not a despised Jew in Nazi Germany. Regarding Nazi treatment of Jews, the American psychologist Diana Baumrind* observes that the "victims were perceived as subhuman and not worthy of consideration."

Finally, as Baumrind notes, it was "obvious from Milgram's own descriptions that most of his subjects were concerned about their victims and did trust the experimenter. Critics therefore claim there is not a convincing parallel between the phenomena studied by Milgram and the destructive obedience that was seen in the subordinate–authority relationship in Hitler's Germany."[5]

Conflict and Consensus

After Milgram's stunning results, researchers repeated the experiment in Germany, South Africa, and Japan. The results revealed similarly high levels of obedience across these different populations, showing that Milgram was wrong in assuming that German culture was defined by a higher-than-average propensity to obey. This, in turn, undermines the argument that higher levels of obedience may have been partly to blame for the Holocaust, unless levels had changed over the intervening 30 years, or unless participants in the studies were not comparable to those who carried out the mass killings.

Baumrind suggests that the laboratory context was unfamiliar and that participants were "more prone to behave in an obedient, suggestible manner in the laboratory than elsewhere." [6] As such, she questions the usefulness of laboratory experiments for gaining a true understanding the factors that make obedience or disobedience more likely to occur in the real world.

Milgram was initially so impressed by the dramatic results in one version of his experiment that he felt the residents of New Haven, and Bridgeport, two cities in the American state of Connecticut, were acting like Nazis. He believed that given the right circumstances, the United States could find individuals to staff concentration camps and extermination sites just as easily as Germany had done. Eventually, he softened his position and stated that the results were purely about obedience as defined by the conditions of his experiment—they should not be used to explain the Holocaust. During an early stage in his work, he had reflected that the work provided better theater than science; at one point, his doubts were so serious that he felt his results were meaningless. Critics agreed with both these conclusions.[7]

NOTES

1 Stanley Milgram, *Obedience to Authority: An Experimental View* (New York: Harper & Row, 1974), 169–70.

2 Milgram, *Obedience to Authority*, 169–78.

3 Jack Katz, *Seductions of Crime: Moral and Sensual Attractions in Doing Evil* (New York: Basic Books, 1988).

4 Milgram, *Obedience to Authority*, 164.

5 Diana Baumrind, "Some Thoughts on the Ethics of Research: After Reading Milgram's 'Behavioral Study of Obedience,'" *American Psychologist* 19, no. 6 (1964): 423.

6 Baumrind, "Some Thoughts," 421.

7 Gina Perry, *Behind the Shock Machine: The Untold Story of the Notorious Milgram Psychology Experiments* (New York: New Press, 2013).

MODULE 10
THE EVOLVING DEBATE

KEY POINTS

- Milgram's work has contributed substantially to Holocaust* scholarship, and has been adapted by other specialties— to enable soldiers to question illegal orders, for example, and to help business people to reject illegal activities.

- Milgram's work built on the ideas of the German American psychologist* Kurt Lewin,* who argued that an individual's behavior always stems from both their personality and the situation in which they find themselves.

- Since Milgram's work was published, scholars have been debating whether his findings can justly be used to explain the Holocaust.

Uses and Problems

Stanley Milgram's results in *Obedience to Authority: An Experimental View* have found numerous practical uses. For instance, business schools have added ethics courses,[1] and business firms are now more likely to urge independent thinking among employees. Some companies now encourage exposure of wrongdoing to the authorities.[2] In the United States, West Point Military Academy's course in military leadership discusses Milgram's work,[3] and US Army training films now include instructions to soldiers on how to disobey illegitimate orders.[4]

One main concern is whether the findings of the original experiments are useful for explaining the Holocaust and similar cases of obedience to unlawful authority. While Milgram suggests that "obedience is the psychological mechanism that links individual action to political purpose,"[5] others are skeptical of applying this claim to extreme situations like the Holocaust.

> ❝ Milgram's work, with its emphasis on the ordinary evils of bureaucracy, made a significant impact on Holocaust scholars that lasts to this day. ❞
>
> K. Fermaglich, *American Dreams and Nazi Nightmares*

In fact, the political theorist Hannah Arendt* argues that "there is no such thing as obedience in political and moral matters."[6] This may sound surprising, coming from the author of the famous 1963 book *Eichmann in Jerusalem: A Report on the Banality of Evil.*[7] This covered the Jerusalem trial of Adolf Eichmann,* the Nazi who had managed the mass deportation and extermination of European Jews during World War II. For Arendt, Eichmann was mainly a bureaucrat who was motivated by a desire to advance his career. For her, obedience alone cannot explain his enormously evil actions; he, like the many others who helped murder the Jews, first had to take the decision to accept the Nazis as a legitimate authority.

While the Danish social scientist* Johannes Lang* has similarly questioned the wisdom of assuming that "individual moral sensibilities are virtually defenseless against situational pressures to conform to such norms,"[8] other scholars think Milgram's work goes far in helping to explain the worst horrors of the twentieth century. The British historian Richard Overy* believes that Milgram's work supports the idea that otherwise good people "can perform horrific acts without necessarily imbibing a hate-filled ideology or being driven by a visceral popular racism."[9]

Schools of Thought

Social psychologists* had long stressed that understanding an individual's unique personality was only part of the process of predicting how that individual might behave in any given circumstance. Indeed, psychologists like Kurt Lewin emphasized the role that situational factors—elements of the social environment—play. Ultimately, Lewin believed that personality and social setting interact to produce a person's behavior in any situation.

By the time he conducted his obedience studies, Milgram was associated with the school of thought pioneered by Lewin. So while his work did not offer an altogether new approach to the field, his research did continue to provide examples of personality and situational factors interacting to explain behavior.

Specifically, Milgram demonstrated that the interaction between the social context created in his laboratory and the personality of the individual resulted in either obedience or disobedience to authority. Many people predicted that only certain types of people would be willing to obey the order to administer painful electric shocks. Indeed, Milgram remarks that some assumed "only Nazis and sadists perform this way."[10] Yet his research indicates just the opposite. By manipulating the appropriate variables in the experiment, he was able to show that "ordinary people no longer perceived themselves as a responsible part of the causal chain leading to action against a person."[11]

In Current Scholarship

Several important books on the Holocaust and human destructiveness make use of Milgram's work: these include Omer Bartov's* *Germany's War and the Holocaust,*[12] David Grossman's* *On Killing: The Psychological Cost of Learning to Kill in War and Society,*[13] Herbert Kelman* and V. Lee Hamilton's* *Crimes of Obedience,*[14] N. J. Kressel's* *Mass Hate: The Global Rise of Genocide and Terror,*[15] F. E. Katz's* *Ordinary People and Extraordinary Evil: A Report on the Beguilings of Evil,*[16] and Zygmunt Bauman's* *Modernity and the Holocaust.*[17]

Richard Overy demonstrates how Milgram's work continues to create debate among those trying to understand exactly what happened during the Holocaust. Milgram's conclusions remain somewhat controversial among "historians … keen to challenge

[Hannah] Arendt and [Stanley] Milgram over the idea that … both obedience to orders and distance from the victim explain how easily they could participate in genocide."[18]

Indeed, some researchers have actually argued that some of the atrocities committed in the Holocaust were originally developed at lower levels of the command chain, and worked themselves back up to the higher authorities.[19]

NOTES

1   O. C. Ferrell and G. Gardiner, *In Pursuit of Ethics: Tough Choices in the World of Work* (Springfield, IL: Smith Collins, 1991).

2   Thomas Blass, *The Man Who Shocked the World: The Life and Legacy of Stanley Milgram* (New York: Basic Books, 2004), 266.

3   Letter from Colonel Howard Prince to Harriet Tobin, April 9, 1964, Stanley Milgram Papers, Manuscripts and Archives, Yale University Library.

4   Blass, *The Man Who Shocked the World,* 278–9.

5   Stanley Milgram, "Behavioral Study of Obedience," *Journal of Abnormal and Social Psychology* 67 (1963): 371.

6   Hannah Arendt, "Auschwitz on Trial," in *Responsibility and Judgment* (New York: Shocken Books, 2003/1964), 17–48.

7   Hannah Arendt, *Eichmann in Jerusalem: A Report on the Banality of Evil* (London: Faber and Faber, 1963).

8   Johannes Lang, "Against Obedience: Hannah Arendt's Overlooked Challenge to Social-Psychological Explanations of Mass Atrocity," *Theory & Psychology* 24, no. 5 (2014): 651.

9   Richard Overy, "'Ordinary Men,' Extraordinary Circumstances: Historians, Social Psychology, and the Holocaust," *Journal of Social Issues* 70, no. 3 (2014): 520.

10   Stanley Milgram, *Obedience to Authority: An Experimental View* (New York: Harper & Row, 1974), 169.

11   Milgram, *Obedience to Authority,* 176.

12   Omer Bartov, *Germany's War and the Holocaust* (Ithaca, NY: Cornell

University Press, 2003).

13 David Grossman, *On Killing: The Psychological Cost of Learning to Kill in War and Society* (Boston: Little, Brown and Company, 1995).

14 Herbert C. Kelman and V. Lee Hamilton, *Crimes of Obedience: Toward a Social Psychology of Authority and Responsibility* (New Haven, CT: Yale University Press, 1989).

15 N. J. Kressel, *Mass Hate: The Global Rise of Genocide and Terror* (Cambridge, MA: Westview Press, 2002).

16 F. E. Katz, *Ordinary People and Extraordinary Evil: A Report on the Beguilings of Evil* (Albany: State University of New York Press, 1993).

17 Z. Bauman, *Modernity and the Holocaust* (Ithaca, NY: Cornell University Press, 1989).

18 Overy, "Ordinary Men," 520.

19 Overy, "Ordinary Men," 520.

MODULE 11
IMPACT AND INFLUENCE TODAY

KEY POINTS

- Milgram's obedience experiments, among the most famous in social psychology,* have been repeated by other researchers and have had a wide influence beyond psychology.*

- According to critics, Milgram exaggerated his findings and suppressed conflicting data.

- Milgram has been accused of designing his experiments (and tweaking them after the first results) to discourage any behaviors that would trigger rebellion.

Position

More than 40 years after its 1974 publication, Stanley Milgram's *Obedience to Authority: An Experimental View* and his experiments "continue to be among the most celebrated in all of social psychology,"[1] and descriptions of Milgram's research are common in introductory psychology texts. The book is both considered a psychology classic and has become popular beyond academia. The research it describes continues to be cited in medical journals, law reviews, and history scholarship.[2] The experiments have been repeated in modified form by more than 20 investigators, in at least nine other countries; the results of these repeat experiments are remarkably consistent.[3]

An appreciation of the harm that can be done by people who are simply following orders, along with insight into the factors that contribute to this sort of behavior, are vitally important for society as a whole. Such knowledge can be used to engineer social institutions in

> **"** The major legacy continues to be the situational thesis that serious harm may be perpetrated upon protesting victims by ordinary good people under the influence of authority. **"**
>
> Arthur G. Miller, "The Explanatory Value of Milgram's Obedience Experiments"

ways that minimize the likelihood of unquestioning obedience to authority that might have harmful consequences.

Milgram's work also changed the ways in which research is conducted. Deception was a necessary element in his studies, and it has been argued that the experiments were ethically questionable. Indeed, many have expressed concern about the stress endured by the participants, and have queried the wisdom of carrying out the experiments in the first place.[4] As a result of "Milgram's studies, the American Psychological Association (APA) formulated its own ethical guidelines and formalized them in 1973."[5] These new guidelines discourage deception unless absolutely necessary and require that any potential stress or discomfort to participants be described in advance. As such, it is very unlikely that Milgram's study would be approved today.

Interaction

Scholars have continued to evaluate the validity of Milgram's methods. The Australian psychologist and journalist Gina Perry,* for example, combed the archives of Milgram's work and interviewed many of his participants and colleagues. She learned that not only had Milgram exaggerated his findings and suppressed conflicting data, but he had allowed many of his participants to leave the lab thinking that they had really harmed someone.

The result of this research was a critical documentary film, and the book *Behind the Shock Machine: The Untold Story of the Notorious*

Milgram Psychology Experiments. These questioned the validity of much of Milgram's work—not just his obedience experiments.[6]

Psychologists became alarmed by the stress experienced by Milgram's volunteers. A number of them apparently suffered for a long time from deep feelings of guilt and shame at having let themselves be pressured into doing what they believed was great harm to another person. The American Psychology Association responded by issuing more stringent guidelines to protect the emotional well-being of participants in experiments. This led, in turn, to the rapid spread of institutional review boards, which now restrict research, especially where deceit and coercion are involved. They now require that volunteers be given a great deal of information about an experiment before participating. The new requirements would have made Milgram's procedures of 1961 impossible today; the study's effectiveness would be eliminated if a volunteer were to discover that the "learner" was not really being shocked.[7]

The Continuing Debate

The debate over Milgram's research continues to the present day. The social psychologist Jolanda Jetten* and political scientist Frank Mols* criticized Milgram's conclusions by arguing that in seeking to minimize rates of disobedience, he used his early observations to change his experimental procedures. Indeed, they suggest that because the experiment "was specifically designed to make people obedient, the finding that they were, hardly tells us anything about the prevalence of such behavior."[8]

Among the factors that Jetten and Mols cite are the incremental nature of the increases in the electric shocks, the delayed protests from the victim, and the prestige associated with Yale University, where much of the research took place.[9] Jetten and Mols further explain, "The context was structured in such a way that it triggered psychological processes known to discourage rebellion: a) division of labor; b) reluctance to contravene rules of politeness; c) absence of a good reason not to continue; d) a novel situation; e) no information about what is normative; f) support for diffusion of responsibility; and g) only limited opportunity to ponder decisions."[10]

The two researchers have even suggested that Milgram may not have actually been studying obedience per se, since the "experimental prod that is most clearly an order ('You have no choice, you must continue') is also least likely to produce obedience."[11] As such they argue that both Milgram's obedient and disobedient participants seemed to want to help the experimenter and to "do the right thing."[12]

NOTES

1   Johannes Lang, "Against Obedience: Hannah Arendt's Overlooked Challenge to Social-Psychological Explanations of Mass Atrocity," *Theory & Psychology* 24, no. 5 (2014): 652.

2   Thomas Blass, *The Man Who Shocked the World: The Life and Legacy of Stanley Milgram* (New York: Basic Books, 2004), 266; and A. M. Perlman, "Unethical Obedience by Subordinate Attorneys: Lessons from Social Psychology," *Hofstra Law Review* 36 (2007): 451–77.

3   Blass, *The Man Who Shocked the World*, 302–3; Lee Ross et al., "History of Social Psychology: Insights, Challenges, and Contributions to Theory and Application," in *Handbook of Social Psychology*, 5th edn, vol. 2, ed. S. T. Fiske et al. (New York: Wiley, 2010), 3–50; and Nester John Charles Russell, "Milgram's Obedience to Authority Experiments: Origins and Early Evolution," *British Journal of Social Psychology* 50 (2011): 140–62.

4   Stanley Milgram, *Obedience to Authority: An Experimental View* (New York: Harper & Row, 1974), 193–202.

5   Katie Youngpeter, "Controversial Psychological Research Methods and Their Influence on the Development of Formal Ethical Guidelines," *Student Journal of Psychological Science* 1, no. 1 (2008), 4–12.

6   Gina Perry, *Behind the Shock Machine: The Untold Story of the Notorious Milgram Psychology Experiments* (New York: New Press, 2013).

7   Youngpeter, "Controversial Psychological Research Methods," 4–12.

8   Jolanda Jetten and Frank Mols, "50:50 Hindsight: Appreciating Anew the Contributions of Milgram's Obedience Experiments," *Journal of Social Issues* 70, no. 3 (2014): 587–602.

9   Jetten and Mols, "50:50 Hindsight," 589.

10   Jetten and Mols, "50:50 Hindsight," 590.

11   Jetten and Mols, "50:50 Hindsight," 590.

12   Jetten and Mols, "50:50 Hindsight," 591.

MODULE 12
WHERE NEXT?

KEY POINTS

- *Obedience to Authority* is likely to remain significant as a summary and discussion of issues regarding conformity* and obedience.

- Identifying basic human tendencies not ordinarily treated elsewhere, the book provides a helpful reference in the study of psychology* and political history; it is especially useful for Holocaust* scholars.

- The book was the first of its kind to detail comprehensively the many conditions under which individuals succumb to authority and override their conscience.

Potential

A discussion of Stanley Milgram's obedience studies in 1974's *Obedience to Authority: An Experimental View* is found in almost all introductory psychology texts; the work is covered in depth by every social psychology* textbook.[1] The extraordinary findings are likely to continue to influence students and their teachers, and to be addressed in psychology classes whenever obedience and conformity are discussed. The studies have been debated in numerous books about the Holocaust since the reports were first published, and have been cited in more than 7,500 scholarly journal articles.[2] There is little sign of their use decreasing.

In popular culture, the 2015 film *Experimenter* suggests a continuing fascination with Milgram's work. Indeed, the psychologists Alexander Haslam* and Stephen Reicher* write that Milgram's research has had such far-reaching effects that it has "spilled over into our general

> **❝ Conformity is often criticized on grounds of morality. Many, if not all, of the greatest human atrocities have been described as 'crimes of obedience.' ❞**
>
> H. C. Kelman and V. L. Hamilton, *Crimes of Obedience*

culture and shaped popular understanding, such that 'everyone knows' that people inevitably succumb to the demands of authority, however immoral the consequences."[3]

The obedience studies are likely to remain somewhat disturbing to most who learn about them for the first time. Such a response is understandable: neither the distress of participants pressured into administering electric shocks nor the darker aspects of human nature revealed by the experiments can be overlooked.

Future Directions

The Canadian psychologist Robert Altemeyer* has suggested several ways in which the kinds of submissiveness that Milgram found, and which scholars have linked to collaboration in Nazi* atrocities, could be prevented.[4] One example would be to include a module in high school civics classes on unjust government actions; he likewise calls for practical training in openly defying authority. Also useful, he says, is teaching about the personality traits described as "authoritarian,"* especially to those who may have authoritarian beliefs. This may "augment their awareness of others."[5]

Examples of nonviolent civil disobedience could be presented to students—for example, through the account of how Mohandas Gandhi* helped lead the Indian independence movement against British rule, and how Martin Luther King, Jr.* helped lead the struggle for civil rights* for African Americans in the United States. History classes could recount the stories of conscientious objectors during World War II* and the Vietnam War,* and devote time to such

movements as the economic equality movement Occupy Wall Street;*
the movement to publicize police violence against African Americans,
Black Lives Matter;* and the Arab Spring,* the popular uprisings in
the Arab world that began in 2010. History and American literature
courses could include modules on the author and political theorist
Henry David Thoreau* and his 1849 essay "Resistance to Civil
Government."

All these approaches could potentially make atrocities like the
Holocaust a little less likely to occur.

Summary

Stanley Milgram's *Obedience to Authority* summarized studies on more
than a thousand participants in a series of psychology experiments. He
observed ordinary people who were asked to administer what they
believed to be painful electric shocks to another person; they were told
this was to test the effects of punishment on learning and memory. The
instructions were intentionally misleading, and the shock generator
was a fake. Readers of these reports were surprised that 40 to 65
percent of participants obeyed the experimenter's demands to
administer a potentially lethal shock of 450 volts to a learner who had
complained of a heart condition. Nevertheless, the willingness of
individuals to obey such commands provided a compelling analogy
for the Holocaust in Europe, during which an untold number of
Germans, Poles, Ukrainians, Romanians, Estonians, and others obeyed
the commands of their leaders to kill more than six million Jews and
members of other marginalized groups.

Milgram and other commentators believed that the results of his
studies provided scientific proof for the existence of a basic tendency
in human nature: to obey established authorities, even when the
actions demanded conflict with personal conscience. Acknowledging
this tendency can help us understand how nonpsychotic, ordinary
people facilitated the monstrous dreams of Germany's leaders. It also

may lend insight into why American military forces massacred noncombatant men, women, and children during the 1960s and 1970s in Vietnam, and why Americans tortured Iraqi prisoners in Iraqi prisons in this century.

If ordinary people can follow orders to hurt their fellow human beings, we need to know what situations and attitudes facilitate such obedience so that we can prevent future atrocities and learn how to help others challenge authority—especially when orders conflict with personal values. Here, in-depth knowledge of the ways in which the study's results differed according to variations in its design can only be beneficial.

NOTES

1   D. Perlman, "Who's Who in Psychology: A Textbook Definition," *American Psychologist* 35 (1980): 104–6; "Recent Developments in Personality and Social Psychology: A Citation Analysis," *Personality and Social Psychology Bulletin* 10 (1984): 492–501.

2   Google Scholar, "Obedience to Authority," accessed May 16, 2016, https://scholar.google.com/scholar?hl=en&q=Obedience+to+Authority+&btnG=&as_sdt=1%2C9&as_sdtp=.

3   S. Alexander Haslam and Stephen D. Reicher, "Contesting the 'Nature' of Conformity: What Milgram and Zimbardo's Studies Really Show," *PLoS Biology* 10, no. 11 (2012): e1001426.

4   Robert Altemeyer, *The Authoritarians*, 2006, accessed May 14, 2016, http://members.chaw.ca/jcanaltemeyer/drbob/TheAuthoritarians.pdf.

5   Altemeyer, *The Authoritarians*, 241.

GLOSSARY

GLOSSARY OF TERMS

Agentic shift: a process that occurs when someone hands over responsibility for their actions to the authority demanding obedience.

Anti-Semitism: prejudice directed toward Jews.

Arab Spring: a series of street demonstrations and civil wars in the Middle East that began in Tunisia in 2010, in the course of which citizens demanded an end to corruption and oppression by overthrowing political leaders.

Authoritarian personality: a cluster of personality traits, including overly submissive tendencies; rigid adherence to rules; intolerance of weakness, sympathy and kindness; excessive admiration for authority and power; intolerance for ambiguity; resistance to personal reflection; prejudice toward members of out-groups; and intense but usually suppressed hostility.

Binding factors: factors that maintain the stability of the social hierarchy.

Black Lives Matter: a grassroots movement in the United States founded in 2012 to protest against the killings by police of unarmed African American citizens, and the various ways in which black people in the United States are denied human rights and dignity.

Roman Catholic Church: the largest and oldest of the Christian denominations. Approximately half of all Christians worldwide are Roman Catholics. Its hierarchical structure has the Pope at its head.

Civil Rights Movement: a social movement in the United States, which peaked in marches, boycotts, and voter-registration drives during the 1960s, aimed at ending racial discrimination and segregation.

Communism: an economic and social system founded on the abolition of class and private industry, in which the people own the resources and tools required for production, and profit is shared between them.

Conformity: the state that occurs when an individual moderates their thought and behavior to be like that of their peers or people of their own status.

Counter-anthropomorphism: the tendency not to recognize human influence in the operation of various institutions.

Cyclon B: a cyanide-based poison gas used in the Nazi death camps to kill large numbers of civilians forced into gas chambers.

Fascism: a type of extreme right-wing government, in place in Italy from 1922 to 1943 and Germany from 1933 to 1945, in which the individual is required to put the interests of the nation above their own, and a dictator rules industry and commerce, forcibly suppressing all dissent.

Holocaust: between 1941 and 1945, over six million European Jews were systematically worked, starved, shot, or gassed to death by the German Nazi regime. More than 200,000 people are estimated to have been directly involved in carrying out the catastrophe in Germany and in German-occupied territories.

In-group: in the social sciences, this refers to the social group to which an individual belongs.

My Lai: a village in the southern portion of Vietnam in which several hundred civilians were killed by American soldiers in 1968.

Nazi Party: an extreme right-wing political party active in Germany from 1920 to 1945; its full name was the Nationalsozialistische Deutsche Arbeiterpartei (the National Socialist German Worker's Party) and it was led by Adolf Hitler. It has been extensively studied by psychologists because of the cruelty and anti-Semitism of its members.

Nuremberg trials: a number of military trials held after World War II in which prominent members of the Nazi Party were prosecuted for war crimes.

Obedience: the action of an individual who complies with authority.

Occupy Wall Street: a protest movement that started in the financial center of New York City during the financial crisis in 2011 and spread internationally. Activists camped out in public parks to publicize the increase in wealth inequality, greed, and corruption, and the influence of corporations on politics.

Out-group: in the social sciences, this refers to any social group to which an individual does not belong.

Peer pressure: the pressure to conform, either in attitudes or behavior, with surrounding people of a similar age or status.

Political science: the study of political behavior and institutions.

Protestantism: a major branch of the Christian religion, formed in the sixteenth century in Germany when reformers broke away from the Roman Catholic Church.

Psychology: the study of the ways in which the mind determines our behavior.

Psychotherapy: a theoretical and therapeutic approach to the understanding of the human mind and behavior, founded on the principle that we are subject to desires and fears held in the unconscious mind.

Social psychology: the field of scholarship and research that investigates how people act in groups, and how their individual behavior is influenced by those around them.

Social responsibility: dependability, trustworthiness, a ready willingness to accept the consequences of one's own behavior; a sense of obligation to wider society.

Third Reich: Germany, from 1933 to 1945, under the rule of the Nazi leader Adolf Hitler. The Third Reich was intended to become as great as the Roman Empire, and last a thousand years.

Totalitarian: when referring to a government, this describes a regime (usually headed by a dictator) that attempts to maintain total control over its citizens.

Vietnam War: a war fought in the years 1955–75 between North Vietnam, with aid from the Soviet Union and China, and South Vietnam, with aid from the United States and its allies.

World War I (1914–18): a global war that saw the United Kingdom, Russia, France, Italy, Japan, and the United States defeat an alliance of Germany, the Austro-Hungarian Empire, and the Ottoman Empire.

World War II (1939–45): a war fought between the Axis powers of Germany, Japan, and Italy, and the Allies, led by Russia, Great Britain, and the United States.

Zeitgeist: the commonly held beliefs and attitudes of a given time period; the word is German and means "the spirit of the time."

PEOPLE MENTIONED IN THE TEXT

Dannie Abse (1923–2014) was a Welsh poet and playwright.

Theodor Adorno (1903–69) was a German social scientist and philosopher.

Gordon W. Allport (1897–1967) was an American psychologist specializing in the study of the personality. He was an important mentor to Stanley Milgram, particularly with his discussion of national characters in his book *The Nature of Prejudice.*

Robert Anthony Altemeyer (b. 1940) is professor emeritus of psychology at the University of Manitoba, where he produced a personality test for right-wing authoritarianism. He focused on the psychology of both authoritarian followers and leaders, and their religious leanings.

Hannah Arendt (1906–75) was a German-born American political theorist who had attended and reported on the trial of Adolf Eichmann, the Nazi who had managed the mass deportation and extermination of Jews during World War II.

Solomon Asch (1907–96) was a pioneer in social psychology in the United States who investigated impression formation, prestige suggestion, and conformity to group pressure.

Omer Bartov (b. 1954) is an Israeli American historian.

Zygmunt Bauman (b. 1927) is a Polish sociologist and an expert on the Holocaust.

Diana Baumrind (b. 1927) is an American psychologist best known for her work on parenting styles.

George Bellak (1919–2002) was an American writer in the television industry.

William Calley (b. 1943) is a former American army officer found guilty of leading his troops in the killing of unarmed civilians in the My Lai massacre in South Vietnam.

Eileen Coughlan is a Canadian author.

Adolf Eichmann (1906–62) was a German Nazi lieutenant colonel who played a major role in organizing the process by which millions of Jews across Europe were stripped of their possessions and transported to their deaths during World War II.

Jerome Frank (1889–1957) was an American legal scholar and federal judge best known for his ideas about how psychological factors come into play in the legal system.

John French (1913–95) was an American psychologist best known for his work on social power, conducted in collaboration with Bertram Raven.

Else Frenkel-Brunswik (1908–58) was an Austrian Polish psychologist who made significant contributions to both social and personality psychology.

Sigmund Freud (1856–1939) was an Austrian neurologist considered the father of psychoanalysis—a therapeutic and theoretical approach that emphasizes the role of the unconscious in patterns of behavior.

Eric Fromm (1900–80) was a German psychologist who made important contributions to the field of social psychology.

Peter Gabriel (b. 1950) is a British singer-songwriter.

Mohandas Gandhi (1869–1948) was an Indian Hindu attorney-activist who pioneered nonviolent civil disobedience, and used it to help lead an independence movement that ended British rule over India.

Daniel Goldhagen (b. 1959) is an American political scientist and author.

David Grossman (b. 1954) is an Israeli author and political activist.

V. Lee Hamilton was an American sociologist.

Adolf Hitler (1889–1945) was chancellor of Germany from 1933 to 1945, supreme commander of the German armed forces from 1938 to 1945, and the politician who provoked and orchestrated the most devastating war in world history, killing approximately 50 million people in Europe, the Atlantic Ocean, and North Africa. More than 10 million died in Asia.

Jolanda Jetten is an Australian social psychologist.

Fred E. Katz is a prominent social scientist and Holocaust survivor.

Jack Katz is an American sociologist best known for his moral seduction theory, which asserts that criminal behavior is motivated by the compelling lure that criminal activity has for the criminal.

Herbert Kelman (b. 1927) is an Austrian American ethicist.

Martin Luther King, Jr. (1929–68) was an African American Baptist minister, holding a PhD from Boston University, who used Gandhi's techniques of nonviolent protest to lead a movement in the 1950s and 1960s to gain civil rights for African Americans in the United States.

N. J. Kressel is an American psychologist who studies various forms of extremism.

Johannes Lang is a Danish social scientist who researches issues related to the Holocaust.

Daniel Levinson (1920–94) was an American psychologist best known for his work on developmental issues in adults.

Kurt Lewin (1890–1947) was a German American psychologist, often recognized as the founder of social psychology, who emphasized that we act within a field of forces that are either driving us toward a goal or hindering us.

Martin Luther (1453–1546) was a Roman Catholic priest who protested against abuses of the Catholic Church, stating that its practices were not consistent with the teachings of Jesus Christ.

Frank Mols is an Australian political scientist.

Richard Overy (b. 1947) is a British historian and expert on World War II.

Gina Perry is an Australian journalist and psychologist.

Bertram Raven (b. 1926) is an American psychologist. He is best known for his work with John French on social power.

Nevitt Sanford (1909–96) was an American psychologist noted for his research on the interactions between personality and social context.

Muzafer Sherif (1906–18) was a Turkish American research scholar who helped found the field of social psychology. His experiments played a key role in showing how much individuals can be influenced by peer pressure.

Shockheaded Peter is a fictional character in a German book of cautionary tales for children who do not follow rules.

Henry David Thoreau (1817–62) was an American author, poet, and philosopher whose writings pioneered civil disobedience as a response to unjust government authority, and served as inspiration for great nonviolent activists of the twentieth century such as Mohandas Gandhi and Martin Luther King, Jr.

Max Weber (1864–1920) was a German social scientist who had considerable influence on the field of social psychology.

WORKS CITED

WORKS CITED

Adorno, Theodor W., Else Frenkel-Brunswik, Daniel J. Levinson, and R. Nevitt Sanford. *The Authoritarian Personality*. New York: Harper, 1950.

Allport, Gordon W. *The Nature of Prejudice.* Reading, MA: Addison-Wesley, 1954.

Altemeyer, Robert. *The Authoritarians.* 2006. Accessed May 14, 2016. http://members.shaw.ca/jeanaltemeyer/drbob/TheAuthoritarians.pdf.

Arendt, Hannah. *Eichmann in Jerusalem: A Report on the Banality of Evil*. London: Faber and Faber, 1963.

On Violence. New York: Harcourt, 1970.

"Auschwitz on Trial." In *Responsibility and Judgment*, 17–48. New York: Schocken Books, 2003.

Asch, Solomon E. *Social Psychology.* Englewood Cliffs, NJ: Prentice-Hall, 1952.

"Studies of Independence and Conformity: I. A Minority of One Against a Unanimous Majority." *Psychological Monographs: General and Applied* 70, no. 9 (1956): 1–70.

Bandura, Albert. "Selective Moral Disengagement in the Exercise of Moral Agency." *Journal of Moral Education* 31, no. 2 (2002): 101–19.

Bartov, Omer. *Germany's War and the Holocaust*: *Disputed Histories*. Ithaca, NY: Cornell University Press, 2003.

Bauman, Z. *Modernity and the Holocaust*. Ithaca, NY: Cornell University Press, 1989.

Baumrind, Diana. "Some Thoughts on the Ethics of Research: After Reading Milgram's 'Behavioral Study of Obedience.'" *American Psychologist* 19, no. 6 (1964): 421–3.

Benjamin, Ludy T., Jr., and Jeffrey A. Simpson. "The Power of the Situation: The Impact of Milgram's Obedience Studies on Personality and Social Psychology." *American Psychologist* 64, no. 1 (2009): 12–19.

Bierstedt, R. "The Problem of Authority." In *Freedom and Control in Modern Society*, edited by M. Berber, T. Abel, and C. Page, 67–81. New York: Van Nostrand, 1954.

Blass, Thomas. *The Man Who Shocked the World: The Life and Legacy of Stanley Milgram*. New York: Basic Books, 2004.

"A Cross-Cultural Comparison of Studies of Obedience Using the Milgram Paradigm: A Review." *Social and Personality Psychology Compass* 6, no. 2 (2012): 196–205.

Brenner, Marie. "The Man Who Knew Too Much." *Vanity Fair*, May 1996. Accessed May 15, 2016. http://www.vanityfair.com/magazine/1996/05/wigand199605.

Burger, J. M. "Situational Variables in Milgram's Experiment That Kept His Participants Shocking." *Journal of Social Issues* 70 (2014): 489–500.

Comfort, Alex. *Authority and Delinquency in the Modern State: A Criminological Approach to the Problem of Power*. London: Routledge and Kegan Paul, 1950.

Fennis, Bob M., and Henk Aarts. "Revisiting the Agentic Shift: Weakening Personal Control Increases Susceptibility to Social Influence." *European Journal of Social Psychology* 42, no. 7 (2012): 824–31.

Fermaglich, K. *American Dreams and Nazi Nightmares: Early Holocaust Consciousness and Liberal America, 1957–1965*. Waltham, MA: Brandeis University Press, 2006.

Ferrell, O. C., and G. Gardiner. *In Pursuit of Ethics: Tough Choices in the World of Work*. Springfield, IL: Smith Collins, 1991.

Frank, Jerome. "Experimental Studies of Personal Pressure and Resistance." *Journal of Genetic Psychology* 30 (1944): 23–64.

French, J. R. P., and B. H. Raven. "The Bases of Social Power." In *Studies in Social Power*, edited by D. Cartwright, 150–67. Ann Arbor: University of Michigan Press, 1959.

Goldhagen, Daniel J. *Hitler's Willing Executioners: Ordinary Germans and the Holocaust*. New York: Little, Brown, 1996.

Grossman, David. *On Killing: The Psychological Cost of Learning to Kill in War and Society*. Boston: Little, Brown and Company, 1995.

Haslam, S. Alexander, and Stephen D. Reicher. "Contesting the 'Nature' of Conformity. What Milgram and Zimbardo's Studies Really Show." *PLoS Biology* 10, no. 11 (2012): e109015. Doi:10.1371/journal.pbio.1001426.

Helm, Charles, and Mario Morelli. "Obedience to Authority in a Laboratory Setting: Generalizability and Context Dependency." *Political Studies* 33 (1985): 610–27.

Jetten, Jolanda, and Frank Mols. "50:50 Hindsight: Appreciating Anew the Contributions of Milgram's Obedience Experiments." *Journal of Social Issues* 70, no. 3 (2014): 587–602.

Katz, F. E. *Ordinary People and Extraordinary Evil: A Report on the Beguilings of Evil*. Albany: State University of New York Press, 1993.

Katz, Jack. *Seductions of Crime: Moral and Sensual Attractions in Doing Evil*. New York: Basic Books, 1988.

Kelman, H., and L. Lawrence. "Assignment of Responsibility in the Case of Lt. Calley: Preliminary Report on a National Survey." *Journal of Social Issues* 28, no. 1 (1972): 177–212.

Kelman, Herbert C., and V. Lee Hamilton. *Crimes of Obedience: Toward a Social Psychology of Authority and Responsibility*. New Haven, CT: Yale University Press, 1989.

Kleinfeld, Judith. "Six Degrees of Separation: Urban Myth?" *Psychology Today* 35, no. 2 (March/April 2002): 74.

Koestler, Arthur. *The Ghost in the Machine*. New York: Macmillan, 1967.

Kressel, N. J. *Mass Hate: The Global Rise of Genocide and Terror.* Boulder, CO: Westview Press, 2002.

Lang, Johannes. "Against Obedience: Hannah Arendt's Overlooked Challenge to Social-Psychological Explanations of Mass Atrocity." *Theory & Psychology* 24, no. 5 (2014): 649–66.

Lewin, Kurt. *Field Theory in Social Science.* New York: Harper & Row, 1951.

Littell, Franklin H. *Hyping the Holocaust: Scholars Answer Goldhagen*. Merion Station, PA: Merion Westfield Press, 1997.

Luther, Martin. "On the Jews and Their Lies." In *The Jew in the Medieval World*, edited by Jacob Marcus, 167–9. New York: Harper Row, 1965.

Mastroianni, George R. "Milgram and the Holocaust: A Reexamination." *Journal of Theoretical and Philosophical Psychology* 22, no. 2 (2002): 158–73.

Milgram, Stanley. "Nationality and Conformity." *Scientific American* 205, no. 6 (1961): 45–51.

"Behavioral Study of Obedience." *Journal of Abnormal and Social Psychology* 67, no. 4 (1963): 371–8.

"Group Pressure and Action Against a Person." *Journal of Abnormal and Social Psychology* 69, no. 2 (1964): 137–43.

"The Small World Problem." *Psychology Today* 1, no. 1 (1967): 60–7.

Obedience to Authority: An Experimental View. New York: Harper & Row, 1974.

The Individual in a Social World: Essays and Experiments. New York: McGraw-Hill, 1992.

Stanley Milgram Papers. Manuscripts and Archives, Yale University Library. Accessed May 16, 2016. http://drs.library.yale.edu/HLTransformer/ HLTransServlet?stylename=yul.ead2002.xhtml.xsl&pid=mssa:ms.1406&query= &clear-stylesheet-cache=yes&hlon=yes&big=&adv=&filter=&hitPageStart=&sor tFields=&view=all.

Milgram, Stanley, and R. L. Shotland, eds. *Television and Antisocial Behavior: Field Experiments*. New York: Academic Press, 1973.

Miller, Arthur G. *The Obedience Experiments: A Case Study of Controversy in Social Science.* New York: Praeger, 1986.

"The Explanatory Value of Milgram's Obedience Experiments: A Contemporary Appraisal." *Journal of Social Issues* 70, no. 3 (2014): 558–73.

Miller, Arthur G., Barry F. Collins, and Diana E. Brief. "Perspectives on Obedience to Authority: The Legacy of the Milgram Experiments." *Journal of Social Issues* 51, no. 3 (1995): 1–19.

Overy, Richard. "'Ordinary Men,' Extraordinary Circumstances: Historians, Social Psychology, and the Holocaust." *Journal of Social Issues* 70, no. 3 (2014): 515–30.

Perlman, A. M. "Unethical Obedience by Subordinate Attorneys: Lessons from Social Psychology." *Hofstra Law Review* 36 (2007): 451–77.

Perlman, D. "Who's Who in Psychology: Endler et al.'s SSCI scores versus a textbook definition." *American Psychologist* 35 (1980): 104–6.

Perry, Gina. *Behind the Shock Machine: The Untold Story of the Notorious Milgram Psychology Experiments.* New York: New Press, 2013.

Ross, Lee, M. Lepper, and A. Ward. "History of Social Psychology: Insights, Challenges, and Contributions to Theory and Application." In *Handbook of Social Psychology,* 5th Edition, Volume 2, edited by S. T. Fiske, D. T. Gilbert, and Gardner Lindzey, 3–50. New York: Wiley, 2010.

Russell, Nester John Charles. "Milgram's Obedience to Authority Experiments: Origins and Early Evolution." *British Journal of Social Psychology* 50 (2011): 140–62.

Sherif, M. "A Study of Some Social Factors in Perception." *Archives of Psychology* 27, no. 187 (1935): 1–60.

Sherif, M., O. Harvey, B. White, W. Hood, and C. Sherif. *Intergroup Conflict and Cooperation: The Robbers Cave Experiment*. Norman: Institute of Group Relations, University of Oklahoma, 1961.

Teather, David. "Spitzer Forces Glaxo to Publish Drug Trials." *Guardian*, August 27, 2004. Accessed May 15, 2016. http://www.theguardian.com/business/2004/aug/27/mentalhealth.glaxosmithklinebusiness.

White, H. "Search for the Parameters of the Small World Phenomenon." *Social Forces* 49, no 2 (1970): 259–64.

Youngpeter, Katie. "Controversial Psychological Research Methods and Their Influence on the Development of Formal Ethical Guidelines." *Student Journal of Psychological Science* 1, no. 1 (2008): 4–12.

THE MACAT LIBRARY
BY DISCIPLINE

AFRICANA STUDIES

Chinua Achebe's *An Image of Africa: Racism in Conrad's Heart of Darkness*
W. E. B. Du Bois's *The Souls of Black Folk*
Zora Neale Huston's *Characteristics of Negro Expression*
Martin Luther King Jr's *Why We Can't Wait*
Toni Morrison's *Playing in the Dark: Whiteness in the American Literary Imagination*

ANTHROPOLOGY

Arjun Appadurai's *Modernity at Large: Cultural Dimensions of Globalisation*
Philippe Ariès's *Centuries of Childhood*
Franz Boas's *Race, Language and Culture*
Kim Chan & Renée Mauborgne's *Blue Ocean Strategy*
Jared Diamond's *Guns, Germs & Steel: the Fate of Human Societies*
Jared Diamond's *Collapse: How Societies Choose to Fail or Survive*
E. E. Evans-Pritchard's *Witchcraft, Oracles and Magic Among the Azande*
James Ferguson's *The Anti-Politics Machine*
Clifford Geertz's *The Interpretation of Cultures*
David Graeber's *Debt: the First 5000 Years*
Karen Ho's *Liquidated: An Ethnography of Wall Street*
Geert Hofstede's *Culture's Consequences: Comparing Values, Behaviors, Institutes and Organizations across Nations*
Claude Lévi-Strauss's *Structural Anthropology*
Jay Macleod's *Ain't No Makin' It: Aspirations and Attainment in a Low-Income Neighborhood*
Saba Mahmood's *The Politics of Piety: The Islamic Revival and the Feminist Subjec*t
Marcel Mauss's *The Gift*

BUSINESS

Jean Lave & Etienne Wenger's *Situated Learning*
Theodore Levitt's *Marketing Myopia*
Burton G. Malkiel's *A Random Walk Down Wall Street*
Douglas McGregor's *The Human Side of Enterprise*
Michael Porter's *Competitive Strategy: Creating and Sustaining Superior Performance*
John Kotter's *Leading Change*
C. K. Prahalad & Gary Hamel's *The Core Competence of the Corporation*

CRIMINOLOGY

Michelle Alexander's *The New Jim Crow: Mass Incarceration in the Age of Colorblindness*
Michael R. Gottfredson & Travis Hirschi's *A General Theory of Crime*
Richard Herrnstein & Charles A. Murray's *The Bell Curve: Intelligence and Class Structure in American Life*
Elizabeth Loftus's *Eyewitness Testimony*
Jay Macleod's *Ain't No Makin' It: Aspirations and Attainment in a Low-Income Neighborhood*
Philip Zimbardo's *The Lucifer Effect*

ECONOMICS

Janet Abu-Lughod's *Before European Hegemony*
Ha-Joon Chang's *Kicking Away the Ladder*
David Brion Davis's *The Problem of Slavery in the Age of Revolution*
Milton Friedman's *The Role of Monetary Policy*
Milton Friedman's *Capitalism and Freedom*
David Graeber's *Debt: the First 5000 Years*
Friedrich Hayek's *The Road to Serfdom*
Karen Ho's *Liquidated: An Ethnography of Wall Street*

John Maynard Keynes's *The General Theory of Employment, Interest and Money*
Charles P. Kindleberger's *Manias, Panics and Crashes*
Robert Lucas's *Why Doesn't Capital Flow from Rich to Poor Countries?*
Burton G. Malkiel's *A Random Walk Down Wall Street*
Thomas Robert Malthus's *An Essay on the Principle of Population*
Karl Marx's *Capital*
Thomas Piketty's *Capital in the Twenty-First Century*
Amartya Sen's *Development as Freedom*
Adam Smith's *The Wealth of Nations*
Nassim Nicholas Taleb's *The Black Swan: The Impact of the Highly Improbable*
Amos Tversky's & Daniel Kahneman's *Judgment under Uncertainty: Heuristics and Biases*
Mahbub Ul Haq's *Reflections on Human Development*
Max Weber's *The Protestant Ethic and the Spirit of Capitalism*

FEMINISM AND GENDER STUDIES

Judith Butler's *Gender Trouble*
Simone De Beauvoir's *The Second Sex*
Michel Foucault's *History of Sexuality*
Betty Friedan's *The Feminine Mystique*
Saba Mahmood's *The Politics of Piety: The Islamic Revival and the Feminist Subjec*t
Joan Wallach Scott's *Gender and the Politics of History*
Mary Wollstonecraft's *A Vindication of the Rights of Woman*
Virginia Woolf's *A Room of One's Own*

GEOGRAPHY

The Brundtland Report's *Our Common Future*
Rachel Carson's *Silent Spring*
Charles Darwin's *On the Origin of Species*
James Ferguson's *The Anti-Politics Machine*
Jane Jacobs's *The Death and Life of Great American Cities*
James Lovelock's *Gaia: A New Look at Life on Earth*
Amartya Sen's *Development as Freedom*
Mathis Wackernagel & William Rees's *Our Ecological Footprint*

HISTORY

Janet Abu-Lughod's *Before European Hegemony*
Benedict Anderson's *Imagined Communities*
Bernard Bailyn's *The Ideological Origins of the American Revolution*
Hanna Batatu's *The Old Social Classes And The Revolutionary Movements Of Iraq*
Christopher Browning's *Ordinary Men: Reserve Police Batallion 101 and the Final Solution in Poland*
Edmund Burke's *Reflections on the Revolution in France*
William Cronon's *Nature's Metropolis: Chicago And The Great West*
Alfred W. Crosby's *The Columbian Exchange*
Hamid Dabashi's *Iran: A People Interrupted*
David Brion Davis's *The Problem of Slavery in the Age of Revolution*
Nathalie Zemon Davis's *The Return of Martin Guerre*
Jared Diamond's *Guns, Germs & Steel: the Fate of Human Societies*
Frank Dikotter's *Mao's Great Famine*
John W Dower's *War Without Mercy: Race And Power In The Pacific War*
W. E. B. Du Bois's *The Souls of Black Folk*
Richard J. Evans's *In Defence of History*
Lucien Febvre's *The Problem of Unbelief in the 16th Century*
Sheila Fitzpatrick's *Everyday Stalinism*

Eric Foner's *Reconstruction: America's Unfinished Revolution, 1863-1877*
Michel Foucault's *Discipline and Punish*
Michel Foucault's *History of Sexuality*
Francis Fukuyama's *The End of History and the Last Man*
John Lewis Gaddis's *We Now Know: Rethinking Cold War History*
Ernest Gellner's *Nations and Nationalism*
Eugene Genovese's *Roll, Jordan, Roll: The World the Slaves Made*
Carlo Ginzburg's *The Night Battles*
Daniel Goldhagen's *Hitler's Willing Executioners*
Jack Goldstone's *Revolution and Rebellion in the Early Modern World*
Antonio Gramsci's *The Prison Notebooks*
Alexander Hamilton, John Jay & James Madison's *The Federalist Papers*
Christopher Hill's *The World Turned Upside Down*
Carole Hillenbrand's *The Crusades: Islamic Perspectives*
Thomas Hobbes's *Leviathan*
Eric Hobsbawm's *The Age Of Revolution*
John A. Hobson's *Imperialism: A Study*
Albert Hourani's *History of the Arab Peoples*
Samuel P. Huntington's *The Clash of Civilizations and the Remaking of World Order*
C. L. R. James's *The Black Jacobins*
Tony Judt's *Postwar: A History of Europe Since 1945*
Ernst Kantorowicz's *The King's Two Bodies: A Study in Medieval Political Theology*
Paul Kennedy's *The Rise and Fall of the Great Powers*
Ian Kershaw's *The "Hitler Myth": Image and Reality in the Third Reich*
John Maynard Keynes's *The General Theory of Employment, Interest and Money*
Charles P. Kindleberger's *Manias, Panics and Crashes*
Martin Luther King Jr's *Why We Can't Wait*
Henry Kissinger's *World Order: Reflections on the Character of Nations and the Course of History*
Thomas Kuhn's *The Structure of Scientific Revolutions*
Georges Lefebvre's *The Coming of the French Revolution*
John Locke's *Two Treatises of Government*
Niccolò Machiavelli's *The Prince*
Thomas Robert Malthus's *An Essay on the Principle of Population*
Mahmood Mamdani's *Citizen and Subject: Contemporary Africa And The Legacy Of Late Colonialism*
Karl Marx's *Capital*
Stanley Milgram's *Obedience to Authority*
John Stuart Mill's *On Liberty*
Thomas Paine's *Common Sense*
Thomas Paine's *Rights of Man*
Geoffrey Parker's *Global Crisis: War, Climate Change and Catastrophe in the Seventeenth Century*
Jonathan Riley-Smith's *The First Crusade and the Idea of Crusading*
Jean-Jacques Rousseau's *The Social Contract*
Joan Wallach Scott's *Gender and the Politics of History*
Theda Skocpol's *States and Social Revolutions*
Adam Smith's *The Wealth of Nations*
Timothy Snyder's *Bloodlands: Europe Between Hitler and Stalin*
Sun Tzu's *The Art of War*
Keith Thomas's *Religion and the Decline of Magic*
Thucydides's *The History of the Peloponnesian War*
Frederick Jackson Turner's *The Significance of the Frontier in American History*
Odd Arne Westad's *The Global Cold War: Third World Interventions And The Making Of Our Times*

LITERATURE

Chinua Achebe's *An Image of Africa: Racism in Conrad's Heart of Darkness*
Roland Barthes's *Mythologies*
Homi K. Bhabha's *The Location of Culture*
Judith Butler's *Gender Trouble*
Simone De Beauvoir's *The Second Sex*
Ferdinand De Saussure's *Course in General Linguistics*
T. S. Eliot's *The Sacred Wood: Essays on Poetry and Criticism*
Zora Neale Huston's *Characteristics of Negro Expression*
Toni Morrison's *Playing in the Dark: Whiteness in the American Literary Imagination*
Edward Said's *Orientalism*
Gayatri Chakravorty Spivak's *Can the Subaltern Speak?*
Mary Wollstonecraft's *A Vindication of the Rights of Women*
Virginia Woolf's *A Room of One's Own*

PHILOSOPHY

Elizabeth Anscombe's *Modern Moral Philosophy*
Hannah Arendt's *The Human Condition*
Aristotle's *Metaphysics*
Aristotle's *Nicomachean Ethics*
Edmund Gettier's *Is Justified True Belief Knowledge?*
Georg Wilhelm Friedrich Hegel's *Phenomenology of Spirit*
David Hume's *Dialogues Concerning Natural Religion*
David Hume's *The Enquiry for Human Understanding*
Immanuel Kant's *Religion within the Boundaries of Mere Reason*
Immanuel Kant's *Critique of Pure Reason*
Søren Kierkegaard's *The Sickness Unto Death*
Søren Kierkegaard's *Fear and Trembling*
C. S. Lewis's *The Abolition of Man*
Alasdair MacIntyre's *After Virtue*
Marcus Aurelius's *Meditations*
Friedrich Nietzsche's *On the Genealogy of Morality*
Friedrich Nietzsche's *Beyond Good and Evil*
Plato's *Republic*
Plato's *Symposium*
Jean-Jacques Rousseau's *The Social Contract*
Gilbert Ryle's *The Concept of Mind*
Baruch Spinoza's *Ethics*
Sun Tzu's *The Art of War*
Ludwig Wittgenstein's *Philosophical Investigations*

POLITICS

Benedict Anderson's *Imagined Communities*
Aristotle's *Politics*
Bernard Bailyn's *The Ideological Origins of the American Revolution*
Edmund Burke's *Reflections on the Revolution in France*
John C. Calhoun's *A Disquisition on Government*
Ha-Joon Chang's *Kicking Away the Ladder*
Hamid Dabashi's *Iran: A People Interrupted*
Hamid Dabashi's *Theology of Discontent: The Ideological Foundation of the Islamic Revolution in Iran*
Robert Dahl's *Democracy and its Critics*
Robert Dahl's *Who Governs?*
David Brion Davis's *The Problem of Slavery in the Age of Revolution*

Alexis De Tocqueville's *Democracy in America*
James Ferguson's *The Anti-Politics Machine*
Frank Dikotter's *Mao's Great Famine*
Sheila Fitzpatrick's *Everyday Stalinism*
Eric Foner's *Reconstruction: America's Unfinished Revolution, 1863-1877*
Milton Friedman's *Capitalism and Freedom*
Francis Fukuyama's *The End of History and the Last Man*
John Lewis Gaddis's *We Now Know: Rethinking Cold War History*
Ernest Gellner's *Nations and Nationalism*
David Graeber's *Debt: the First 5000 Years*
Antonio Gramsci's *The Prison Notebooks*
Alexander Hamilton, John Jay & James Madison's *The Federalist Papers*
Friedrich Hayek's *The Road to Serfdom*
Christopher Hill's *The World Turned Upside Down*
Thomas Hobbes's *Leviathan*
John A. Hobson's *Imperialism: A Study*
Samuel P. Huntington's *The Clash of Civilizations and the Remaking of World Order*
Tony Judt's *Postwar: A History of Europe Since 1945*
David C. Kang's *China Rising: Peace, Power and Order in East Asia*
Paul Kennedy's *The Rise and Fall of Great Powers*
Robert Keohane's *After Hegemony*
Martin Luther King Jr.'s *Why We Can't Wait*
Henry Kissinger's *World Order: Reflections on the Character of Nations and the Course of History*
John Locke's *Two Treatises of Government*
Niccolò Machiavelli's *The Prince*
Thomas Robert Malthus's *An Essay on the Principle of Population*
Mahmood Mamdani's *Citizen and Subject: Contemporary Africa And The Legacy Of Late Colonialism*
Karl Marx's *Capital*
John Stuart Mill's *On Liberty*
John Stuart Mill's *Utilitarianism*
Hans Morgenthau's *Politics Among Nations*
Thomas Paine's *Common Sense*
Thomas Paine's *Rights of Man*
Thomas Piketty's *Capital in the Twenty-First Century*
Robert D. Putman's *Bowling Alone*
John Rawls's *Theory of Justice*
Jean-Jacques Rousseau's *The Social Contract*
Theda Skocpol's *States and Social Revolutions*
Adam Smith's *The Wealth of Nations*
Sun Tzu's *The Art of War*
Henry David Thoreau's *Civil Disobedience*
Thucydides's *The History of the Peloponnesian War*
Kenneth Waltz's *Theory of International Politics*
Max Weber's *Politics as a Vocation*
Odd Arne Westad's *The Global Cold War: Third World Interventions And The Making Of Our Times*

POSTCOLONIAL STUDIES

Roland Barthes's *Mythologies*
Frantz Fanon's *Black Skin, White Masks*
Homi K. Bhabha's *The Location of Culture*
Gustavo Gutiérrez's *A Theology of Liberation*
Edward Said's *Orientalism*
Gayatri Chakravorty Spivak's *Can the Subaltern Speak?*

PSYCHOLOGY

Gordon Allport's *The Nature of Prejudice*
Alan Baddeley & Graham Hitch's *Aggression: A Social Learning Analysis*
Albert Bandura's *Aggression: A Social Learning Analysis*
Leon Festinger's *A Theory of Cognitive Dissonance*
Sigmund Freud's *The Interpretation of Dreams*
Betty Friedan's *The Feminine Mystique*
Michael R. Gottfredson & Travis Hirschi's *A General Theory of Crime*
Eric Hoffer's *The True Believer: Thoughts on the Nature of Mass Movements*
William James's *Principles of Psychology*
Elizabeth Loftus's *Eyewitness Testimony*
A. H. Maslow's *A Theory of Human Motivation*
Stanley Milgram's *Obedience to Authority*
Steven Pinker's *The Better Angels of Our Nature*
Oliver Sacks's *The Man Who Mistook His Wife For a Hat*
Richard Thaler & Cass Sunstein's *Nudge: Improving Decisions About Health, Wealth and Happiness*
Amos Tversky's *Judgment under Uncertainty: Heuristics and Biases*
Philip Zimbardo's *The Lucifer Effect*

SCIENCE

Rachel Carson's *Silent Spring*
William Cronon's *Nature's Metropolis: Chicago And The Great West*
Alfred W. Crosby's *The Columbian Exchange*
Charles Darwin's *On the Origin of Species*
Richard Dawkin's *The Selfish Gene*
Thomas Kuhn's *The Structure of Scientific Revolutions*
Geoffrey Parker's *Global Crisis: War, Climate Change and Catastrophe in the Seventeenth Century*
Mathis Wackernagel & William Rees's *Our Ecological Footprint*

SOCIOLOGY

Michelle Alexander's *The New Jim Crow: Mass Incarceration in the Age of Colorblindness*
Gordon Allport's *The Nature of Prejudice*
Albert Bandura's *Aggression: A Social Learning Analysis*
Hanna Batatu's *The Old Social Classes And The Revolutionary Movements Of Iraq*
Ha-Joon Chang's *Kicking Away the Ladder*
W. E. B. Du Bois's *The Souls of Black Folk*
Émile Durkheim's *On Suicide*
Frantz Fanon's *Black Skin, White Masks*
Frantz Fanon's *The Wretched of the Earth*
Eric Foner's *Reconstruction: America's Unfinished Revolution, 1863-1877*
Eugene Genovese's *Roll, Jordan, Roll: The World the Slaves Made*
Jack Goldstone's *Revolution and Rebellion in the Early Modern World*
Antonio Gramsci's *The Prison Notebooks*
Richard Herrnstein & Charles A Murray's *The Bell Curve: Intelligence and Class Structure in American Life*
Eric Hoffer's *The True Believer: Thoughts on the Nature of Mass Movements*
Jane Jacobs's *The Death and Life of Great American Cities*
Robert Lucas's *Why Doesn't Capital Flow from Rich to Poor Countries?*
Jay Macleod's *Ain't No Makin' It: Aspirations and Attainment in a Low Income Neighborhood*
Elaine May's *Homeward Bound: American Families in the Cold War Era*
Douglas McGregor's *The Human Side of Enterprise*
C. Wright Mills's *The Sociological Imagination*

Thomas Piketty's *Capital in the Twenty-First Century*
Robert D. Putman's *Bowling Alone*
David Riesman's *The Lonely Crowd: A Study of the Changing American Character*
Edward Said's *Orientalism*
Joan Wallach Scott's *Gender and the Politics of History*
Theda Skocpol's *States and Social Revolutions*
Max Weber's *The Protestant Ethic and the Spirit of Capitalism*

THEOLOGY

Augustine's *Confessions*
Benedict's *Rule of St Benedict*
Gustavo Gutiérrez's *A Theology of Liberation*
Carole Hillenbrand's *The Crusades: Islamic Perspectives*
David Hume's *Dialogues Concerning Natural Religion*
Immanuel Kant's *Religion within the Boundaries of Mere Reason*
Ernst Kantorowicz's *The King's Two Bodies: A Study in Medieval Political Theology*
Søren Kierkegaard's *The Sickness Unto Death*
C. S. Lewis's *The Abolition of Man*
Saba Mahmood's *The Politics of Piety: The Islamic Revival and the Feminist Subject*
Baruch Spinoza's *Ethics*
Keith Thomas's *Religion and the Decline of Magic*

COMING SOON

Chris Argyris's *The Individual and the Organisation*
Seyla Benhabib's *The Rights of Others*
Walter Benjamin's *The Work Of Art in the Age of Mechanical Reproduction*
John Berger's *Ways of Seeing*
Pierre Bourdieu's *Outline of a Theory of Practice*
Mary Douglas's *Purity and Danger*
Roland Dworkin's *Taking Rights Seriously*
James G. March's *Exploration and Exploitation in Organisational Learning*
Ikujiro Nonaka's *A Dynamic Theory of Organizational Knowledge Creation*
Griselda Pollock's *Vision and Difference*
Amartya Sen's *Inequality Re-Examined*
Susan Sontag's *On Photography*
Yasser Tabbaa's *The Transformation of Islamic Art*
Ludwig von Mises's *Theory of Money and Credit*

Macat Disciplines

Access the greatest ideas and thinkers across entire disciplines, including

Postcolonial Studies

Roland Barthes's *Mythologies*
Frantz Fanon's *Black Skin, White Masks*
Homi K. Bhabha's *The Location of Culture*
Gustavo Gutiérrez's *A Theology of Liberation*
Edward Said's *Orientalism*
Gayatri Chakravorty Spivak's *Can the Subaltern Speak?*

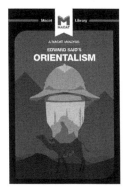

Macat analyses are available from all good bookshops and libraries.

Access hundreds of analyses through one, multimedia tool.
Join free for one month **library.macat.com**

Macat Disciplines

Access the greatest ideas and thinkers across entire disciplines, including

AFRICANA STUDIES

Chinua Achebe's *An Image of Africa: Racism in Conrad's Heart of Darkness*

W. E. B. Du Bois's *The Souls of Black Folk*

Zora Neale Hurston's *Characteristics of Negro Expression*

Martin Luther King Jr.'s *Why We Can't Wait*

Toni Morrison's *Playing in the Dark: Whiteness in the American Literary Imagination*

Macat analyses are available from all good bookshops and libraries.

Access hundreds of analyses through one, multimedia tool.
Join free for one month **library.macat.com**

Macat Disciplines

Access the greatest ideas and thinkers across entire disciplines, including

FEMINISM, GENDER AND QUEER STUDIES

Simone De Beauvoir's
The Second Sex

Michel Foucault's
History of Sexuality

Betty Friedan's
The Feminine Mystique

Saba Mahmood's
*The Politics of Piety:
The Islamic Revival and
the Feminist Subject*

Joan Wallach Scott's
*Gender and the
Politics of History*

Mary Wollstonecraft's
*A Vindication of the
Rights of Woman*

Virginia Woolf's
A Room of One's Own

Judith Butler's
Gender Trouble

Macat analyses are available from all good bookshops and libraries.

Access hundreds of analyses through one, multimedia tool.
Join free for one month **library.macat.com**

Macat Disciplines

*Access the greatest ideas and thinkers
across entire disciplines, including*

CRIMINOLOGY

Michelle Alexander's
*The New Jim Crow:
Mass Incarceration in the
Age of Colorblindness*

**Michael R. Gottfredson
& Travis Hirschi's**
A General Theory of Crime

Elizabeth Loftus's
Eyewitness Testimony

**Richard Herrnstein
& Charles A. Murray's**
*The Bell Curve: Intelligence and
Class Structure in American Life*

Jay Macleod's
*Ain't No Makin' It:
Aspirations and Attainment in a
Low-Income Neighborhood*

Philip Zimbardo's
The Lucifer Effect

Macat Disciplines

Access the greatest ideas and thinkers across entire disciplines, including

INEQUALITY

Ha-Joon Chang's, *Kicking Away the Ladder*

David Graeber's, *Debt: The First 5000 Years*

Robert E. Lucas's, *Why Doesn't Capital Flow from Rich To Poor Countries?*

Thomas Piketty's, *Capital in the Twenty-First Century*

Amartya Sen's, *Inequality Re-Examined*

Mahbub Ul Haq's, *Reflections on Human Development*

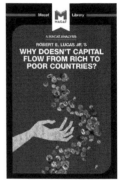

Macat analyses are available from all good bookshops and libraries.

Access hundreds of analyses through one, multimedia tool.
Join free for one month **library.macat.com**

Macat Disciplines

Access the greatest ideas and thinkers across entire disciplines, including

GLOBALIZATION

Arjun Appadurai's, *Modernity at Large: Cultural Dimensions of Globalisation*

James Ferguson's, *The Anti-Politics Machine*

Geert Hofstede's, *Culture's Consequences*

Amartya Sen's, *Development as Freedom*

Macat Disciplines

Access the greatest ideas and thinkers across entire disciplines, including

MAN AND THE ENVIRONMENT

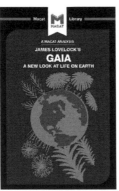

The Brundtland Report's, *Our Common Future*

Rachel Carson's, *Silent Spring*

James Lovelock's, *Gaia: A New Look at Life on Earth*

Mathis Wackernagel & William Rees's, *Our Ecological Footprint*

Macat Disciplines

Access the greatest ideas and thinkers across entire disciplines, including

THE FUTURE OF DEMOCRACY

Robert A. Dahl's, *Democracy and Its Critics*
Robert A. Dahl's, *Who Governs?*
Alexis De Toqueville's, *Democracy in America*
Niccolò Machiavelli's, *The Prince*
John Stuart Mill's, *On Liberty*
Robert D. Putnam's, *Bowling Alone*
Jean-Jacques Rousseau's, *The Social Contract*
Henry David Thoreau's, *Civil Disobedience*

Macat Disciplines

Access the greatest ideas and thinkers across entire disciplines, including

TOTALITARIANISM

Sheila Fitzpatrick's, *Everyday Stalinism*
Ian Kershaw's, *The "Hitler Myth"*
Timothy Snyder's, *Bloodlands*

Macat Pairs

Analyse historical and modern issues from opposite sides of an argument. Pairs include:

RACE AND IDENTITY

Zora Neale Hurston's
Characteristics of Negro Expression

Using material collected on anthropological expeditions to the South, Zora Neale Hurston explains how expression in African American culture in the early twentieth century departs from the art of white America. At the time, African American art was often criticized for copying white culture. For Hurston, this criticism misunderstood how art works. European tradition views art as something fixed. But Hurston describes a creative process that is alive, ever-changing, and largely improvisational. She maintains that African American art works through a process called 'mimicry'—where an imitated object or verbal pattern, for example, is reshaped and altered until it becomes something new, novel—and worthy of attention.

Frantz Fanon's
Black Skin, White Masks

Black Skin, White Masks offers a radical analysis of the psychological effects of colonization on the colonized.

Fanon witnessed the effects of colonization first hand both in his birthplace, Martinique, and again later in life when he worked as a psychiatrist in another French colony, Algeria. His text is uncompromising in form and argument. He dissects the dehumanizing effects of colonialism, arguing that it destroys the native sense of identity, forcing people to adapt to an alien set of values—including a core belief that they are inferior. This results in deep psychological trauma.

Fanon's work played a pivotal role in the civil rights movements of the 1960s.

Macat analyses are available from all good bookshops and libraries.

Access hundreds of analyses through one, multimedia tool.
Join free for one month **library.macat.com**

Macat Pairs

Analyse historical and modern issues from opposite sides of an argument. Pairs include:

INTERNATIONAL RELATIONS IN THE 21ST CENTURY

Samuel P. Huntington's
The Clash of Civilisations

In his highly influential 1996 book, Huntington offers a vision of a post-Cold War world in which conflict takes place not between competing ideologies but between cultures. The worst clash, he argues, will be between the Islamic world and the West: the West's arrogance and belief that its culture is a "gift" to the world will come into conflict with Islam's obstinacy and concern that its culture is under attack from a morally decadent "other."

Clash inspired much debate between different political schools of thought. But its greatest impact came in helping define American foreign policy in the wake of the 2001 terrorist attacks in New York and Washington.

Francis Fukuyama's
The End of History and the Last Man

Published in 1992, *The End of History and the Last Man* argues that capitalist democracy is the final destination for all societies. Fukuyama believed democracy triumphed during the Cold War because it lacks the "fundamental contradictions" inherent in communism and satisfies our yearning for freedom and equality. Democracy therefore marks the endpoint in the evolution of ideology, and so the "end of history." There will still be "events," but no fundamental change in ideology.

Macat Pairs

Analyse historical and modern issues from opposite sides of an argument. Pairs include:

HOW TO RUN AN ECONOMY

John Maynard Keynes's
The General Theory OF Employment, Interest and Money

Classical economics suggests that market economies are self-correcting in times of recession or depression, and tend toward full employment and output. But English economist John Maynard Keynes disagrees.

In his ground-breaking 1936 study *The General Theory*, Keynes argues that traditional economics has misunderstood the causes of unemployment. Employment is not determined by the price of labor; it is directly linked to demand. Keynes believes market economies are by nature unstable, and so require government intervention. Spurred on by the social catastrophe of the Great Depression of the 1930s, he sets out to revolutionize the way the world thinks

Milton Friedman's
The Role of Monetary Policy

Friedman's 1968 paper changed the course of economic theory. In just 17 pages, he demolished existing theory and outlined an effective alternate monetary policy designed to secure 'high employment, stable prices and rapid growth.'

Friedman demonstrated that monetary policy plays a vital role in broader economic stability and argued that economists got their monetary policy wrong in the 1950s and 1960s by misunderstanding the relationship between inflation and unemployment. Previous generations of economists had believed that governments could permanently decrease unemployment by permitting inflation—and vice versa. Friedman's most original contribution was to show that this supposed trade-off is an illusion that only works in the short term.

Macat analyses are available from all good bookshops and libraries.

Access hundreds of analyses through one, multimedia tool.
Join free for one month **library.macat.com**

Macat Pairs

Analyse historical and modern issues from opposite sides of an argument. Pairs include:

Macat Pairs

Analyse historical and modern issues from opposite sides of an argument. Pairs include:

HOW WE RELATE TO EACH OTHER AND SOCIETY

Jean-Jacques Rousseau's
The Social Contract

Rousseau's famous work sets out the radical concept of the 'social contract': a give-and-take relationship between individual freedom and social order.

If people are free to do as they like, governed only by their own sense of justice, they are also vulnerable to chaos and violence. To avoid this, Rousseau proposes, they should agree to give up some freedom to benefit from the protection of social and political organization. But this deal is only just if societies are led by the collective needs and desires of the people, and able to control the private interests of individuals. For Rousseau, the only legitimate form of government is rule by the people.

Robert D. Putnam's
Bowling Alone

In *Bowling Alone*, Robert Putnam argues that Americans have become disconnected from one another and from the institutions of their common life, and investigates the consequences of this change.

Looking at a range of indicators, from membership in formal organizations to the number of invitations being extended to informal dinner parties, Putnam demonstrates that Americans are interacting less and creating less "social capital" – with potentially disastrous implications for their society.

It would be difficult to overstate the impact of *Bowling Alone*, one of the most frequently cited social science publications of the last half-century.

Macat analyses are available from all good bookshops and libraries.

Access hundreds of analyses through one, multimedia tool.
Join free for one month **library.macat.com**

For Product Safety Concerns and Information please contact our EU
representative GPSR@taylorandfrancis.com Taylor & Francis Verlag GmbH,
Kaufingerstraße 24, 80331 München, Germany

Printed and bound by CPI Group (UK) Ltd, Croydon, CR0 4YY
11/04/2025
01844003-0001